BREAKFAST INN STYLE

BREAKFAST INN STYLE

Historic and Romantic
Inns of the Southeast
and Their Signature Recipes

Barbara M. Wohlford
AND Mary L. Eley

RUTLEDGE HILL PRESS
Nashville, Tennessee

Published in Nashville, Tennessee, by Rutledge Hill Press, Inc., 211 Seventh Avenue North, Nashville, Tennessee 37219. Distributed in Canada by H. B. Fenn & Company, Ltd., 34 Nixon Road, Bolton, Ontario L7E 1W2. Distributed in Australia by Millenium Books, 33 Maddox Street, Alexandria, NSW 2015. Distributed in New Zealand by Tandem Press, 2 Rugby Road, Birkenhead, Aukland 10. Distributed in the United Kingdom by Verulam Publishing, Ltd., 152a Park Street Lane, Park Street, St. Albans, Hertfordshire AL2 2AU.

Illustrations by Janet Brooks or supplied by inns
Cover and book design by Harriette Bateman
Typography by D&T/Bailey Typesetting, Inc., Nashville, Tennessee

Library of Congress Cataloging-in-Publication Data

Wohlford, Barbara M.
    Breakfast inn style : historic and romantic inns of the Southeast and their signature recipes / Barbara M. Wohlford and Mary L. Eley.
        p.   cm.
    Includes index.
    ISBN 1-55853-463-6 (pbk.)
    1. Breakfasts.   2. Bed and breakfast accommodations—Southern States—Guidebooks.   3. Hotels—Southern States—Guidebooks.
I. Eley, Mary L.   II. Title.
TX733.W65   1997
647.9475'03—dc21   97-425
                                                                         CIP

Printed in the United States of America
1 2 3 4 5 6 7 8 9—01 00 99 98 97

CONTENTS

We would like to express our appreciation to all the
wonderful cooks and recipe testers who volunteered to be
a part of our project. Your evaluations helped ensure that
the recipes selected for this book are delectable, enticing,
and fun to prepare for family and fortunate guests.

We would also like to thank our editor, Charla Honea,
for her ideas, help, and encouragement.

Thanks also to our husbands, Jack Wohlford and Claude Eley,
who willingly consumed more versions of French Toast
than they ever dreamed possible.

Barbara M. Wohlford
and
Mary L. Eley

$\mathscr{I}$NTRODUCTION

$\mathscr{W}$e first tasted the charms of B&B homes and Country Inns while traveling in our home state of Virginia. In an age of homogenization, here was individuality! Whatever their location, B&Bs and Country Inns are the personal statements of their owners. They provide an inviting combination of homey comforts, good conversation and fabulous food. Each establishment offers its distinctive touches—fresh flowers in your room every day or wine and cheese served on a silver tray beside a warming fire—that reflect attentive service and dedication to details. In today's B&B and Country Inn, the time-honored traditions of hospitality await every traveler.

We focus here on the B&Bs and Country Inns of the Southeast, a region of exceptional beauty, with strong ties to the history of the nation. Many of the homes and inns we have selected are listed on the National Register of Historic Places. Some are located in picturesque mountain spots or beside romantic coastal shores. Some are near attractions of special significance. Each offers a setting as unique as the personality of your host, from the nostalgic appeal of antique furnishings and hand-sewn quilts on every bed to the flair of contemporary design. But whatever their style, they all assure the guest of old-fashioned graciousness, Southern gentility, and superb cuisine.

Any visit to a B&B home or Country Inn should include the surrounding area. To facilitate your planning, we have included descriptions of attractions and activities—mountain and beach locales, parks, recreation areas, historic sites, shopping and "antique-ing" opportunities.

As you plan your trip, remember that there is wide variation from inn to inn—rates, number of rooms, availability of private baths and other amenities. Some places welcome children; others do not. Smoking may or may not be permitted. Some will provide for pets; others will not. You should always call for reservations in advance and be sure that the accommodations offered meet your requirements. Once you have made your arrangements, it's time to dust off your spirit of adventure, pack your bags, work up a healthy appetite—and prepare to be pampered.

The B&Bs and Country Inns included in *Breakfast Inn Style* have generously shared some of their favorite recipes for your enjoyment. Each recipe has been tested for taste, ease of preparation, availability of ingredients, and presentation. We have included hints from the chefs where possible, and added some of our own tips as well. You will find dishes that are very easy to prepare and some that are more complicated, but we can assure you that every recipe is deliciously worth your time.

In researching this book, we were reminded of a timeless truth that is sometimes overlooked in the modern rush. The basic ingredients for a memorable breakfast, brunch or afternoon tea are well-prepared food, served with panache and sprinkled with lively conversation. The recipes we offer here come from some of the Southeast's best B&B and Country Inn kitchens, where the preparation of food is integral to the art of gracious hospitality. Our sample menus will help you easily assemble meals that become occasions for everyone. Just add freshly squeezed fruit juice, steaming coffee or your favorite drinks . . . and savor the tastes of the Southeast.

BARBARA M. WOHLFORD
MARY L. ELEY

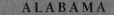

ROSES & LACE COUNTRY INN

P. O. Box 852 • Ashville, Alabama 35953 • (205) 594-4366 • Wayne and Faye Payne

Wayne and Faye Payne have carefully blended the elegance of by-gone days with modern amenities in their handsomely restored Queen Anne-style home. Long known as the Robinson Montgomery House, the inn was built in 1890 by Judge E. J. Robinson, a Civil War veteran, and is now listed on the National Register of Historic Places. The name has been changed to Roses & Lace, but the house retains many of its original features including rich heart pine woodwork, colorful stained glass windows, and sparkling crystal chandeliers.

Roses & Lace Country Inn offers four spacious and beautifully appointed guest bedrooms. A stay with the Paynes includes a full Southern breakfast. Dinner can be provided at extra cost and with reservations. Smoking is not permitted.

Ashville and its surrounding area offers rich hunting grounds for antique lovers. Sites of interest in the town include the historic Ashville Courthouse and the local library. Ashville is a comfortable 45-mile drive from Birmingham and 80 miles from Huntsville, where visitors can see space-age history on display at the Space and Rocket Center. After a day of touring and shopping, we recommend that you retreat to the shelter of the verandah at the Roses & Lace and relax Southern-style with a glass of iced tea and home-baked cookies.

*F*RESH APPLE CAKE

Cake
- 1 cup sugar
- ¾ cup oil
- 2 eggs
- 1½ cups chopped Rome apples
- 1 cup chopped nuts
- 1 teaspoon vanilla extract
- 1½ cups self-rising flour
- 1 teaspoon cinnamon

Topping
- ½ cup butter (1 stick)
- 1 cup firmly packed light brown sugar
- 1 teaspoon vanilla extract
- ¼ cup evaporated milk

Prepare the cake. In a mixing bowl, cream together the sugar and the oil. Add the eggs, one at a time. Add the apples and nuts; then mix in the vanilla, flour, and cinnamon. Bake in a greased and floured tube pan at 325° for 40 minutes. Allow the cake to cool in the pan for 5 to 10 minutes before removing. Place on a wire rack.

To prepare the topping, in a small saucepan heat the butter and sugar, stirring until thoroughly mixed. Add the vanilla and milk. Stir until cool and pour over the cake.

SERVES 12.

*W*OOD AVENUE INN

658 North Wood Avenue • Florence, Alabama 35630 • (205) 766-8441 • Gene and Alvern Greeley

*G*uests will find much to see and do in this charming northern Alabama town, whose sister city in Italy was the wellspring of the Renaissance. The historic district of Florence, Alabama, includes the Wood Avenue Inn, a gracious Queen Anne mansion built in 1889. In classic Victorian style, the home includes both square and octagonal towers, ten fireplaces, and 14-foot ceilings. Its wraparound porch is an inviting setting for relaxation and contemplation after a busy day of exploring the city. You will also enjoy the mansion's many antique furnishings. Guests at Wood Avenue Inn have a special treat in store each morning—a full English breakfast served at a quiet candle-lit table to the accompaniment of soft music. What a harmonious start to the day!

FRESH STRAWBERRY CRÊPES

1 cup all-purpose flour
1⅔ cups milk
1½ tablespoons oil
2 eggs
½ teaspoon salt
1½ cups nondairy whipped topping

1 cup sour cream
1½ tablespoons powdered sugar
1 teaspoon vanilla extract
Fresh strawberries
Shaved almonds

To make the crêpes, combine the flour, milk, oil, eggs, and salt in a blender and blend for 1½ minutes. Allow to sit overnight. The next day, make a cream filling for the crêpes by combining the whipped topping, sour cream, powdered sugar, and vanilla. To assemble crêpes, grease and heat a 5-inch skillet with a few drops of oil or spray skillet with a non-stick cooking spray. Add and melt a small quantity of butter in the skillet. Pour in just enough batter to thinly coat the bottom of the pan. Cook the crêpe over moderate heat. When the underside is a light brown color, flip it over and lightly brown the other side of the crêpe. Place 2 tablespoons of the cream filling on each crêpe. Fold the crêpe so that the seam is underneath. Cover the crêpes with fresh strawberries and garnish with shaved almonds.

MAKES 8 CRÊPES OR 4 SERVINGS.

Chef's Hint: Serve with fresh juice, strong coffee, and soft harp music.

GRACE HALL BED & BREAKFAST

506 Lauderdale Street • Selma, Alabama 36701 • (334) 875-5744 • Joey and Coy Dillon

It was in 1863, from the porch of Grace Hall, that Madison Jackson Williams, mayor of the town, sent his home guard off to fight what became the last battle of the Confederacy. The battle was lost, but Grace Hall was saved from burning when Union Soldiers occupied Selma. Built circa 1857, the house later became the most fashionable boarding facility in the town. Miss Grace Hall, for whom the house was named, was born in the Green Room on October 4, 1898.

Condemned in 1978, Grace Hall was saved from destruction once more when it purchased by Joey Dillon in 1981. After five years of restoration, the Hall was brought back to its original glory. It is now listed on the National Register of Historic Places, and the restoration is certified by the U.S. Department of the Interior.

This history-drenched Southern mansion offers six guest rooms, and rates include a tour of the mansion, morning coffee, and a full breakfast.

Just 45-minutes' drive from Montgomery, Selma was once the heart of Alabama's cotton culture and includes the largest historic district in the state, with more than 1,200 structures. Visitors will find palatial antebellum homes and stately Victorians, as well as a wealth of antique stores and Victorian cottage shops where hand-crafted items are a specialty. While in Selma, you will want to visit the Edmund Pettus Bridge, site of the dramatic clash during the 1965 Civil Rights march to Montgomery led by Dr. Martin Luther King, Jr. It was in Brown Chapel A. M. E. Church that Dr. King launched the march. Selma hosts a variety of annual events including an historic homes tour, Civil War re-enactment, catfish cookout, and storytellers' gathering.

GRACE HALL COFFEE CAKE

Cake
- 8 ounces butter (2 sticks)
- 2 cups sugar
- 1 pound sour cream
- 2 teaspoons baking soda
- 4 eggs
- 2 teaspoons vanilla extract
- 3 cups sifted all-purpose flour
- 2 teaspoons baking powder

Topping
- ½ cup sugar
- 2 teaspoons cinnamon
- ½ cup chopped nuts

Grease a 15x10x2-inch pan. Preheat oven to 350°. In a mixing bowl, cream together the butter and sugar. Add the sour cream, baking soda, and eggs, one at a time. Beat well and stir in the vanilla. Mix the baking powder into the flour. Add the butter-sugar mixture to the flour mixture. Stir just until blended, then pour into the greased pan. Prepare the topping by combining the sugar, cinnamon, and chopped nuts. Sprinkle the topping on top of cake and gently cut it into the batter. Bake at 350° for 45 minutes. May be frozen and served later.

SERVES 20.

CHALET SUZANNE

3800 Chalet Suzanne Drive • Lake Wales, Florida 33853 • (813) 676-6011 or (800) 433-6011 •
Carl and Vita Hinshaw

This enchanting 30-room inn has been featured in *Country Inns of the Old South* and is listed on the National Register of Historic Places. Nestled in a 70-acre estate amid the exciting attractions of Orlando and Central Florida, Chalet Suzanne is a feast for the eyes and the appetite. Years of expansion have created a multi-leveled facility where walls may be out of plumb, floors slope oddly, and rooms are proportioned to suit both Gulliver and the Lilliputians. One room has three wash basins; another features a sunken shower made of Middle Eastern tiles. The "Honeymoon Suite" inspires Medieval fantasies with its draped bed, balcony and Moorish glass lantern, and a dumb waiter stands ready to deliver meals directly to the suite's occupants. The inn's pool, sparkling lake and even a landing strip are just steps from your courtyard or patio.

Renowned for its cuisine, the Chalet's award-winning restaurant has been voted one of Florida's top ten for more than two decades. Be sure to try Chalet Suzanne's famous home-made soups during your stay. They're literally "out of this world." Astronaut James Irwin enjoyed the soup so much that it traveled with the crew of Apollo 15 on their 1973 moon trip. Carl Hinshaw's soups were also aboard Apollo 16, and were enjoyed by the astronauts of the joint Russian and American Apollo-Soyez mission. Today, they are sold and shipped worldwide.

Wonderfully situated for Florida touring, Chalet Suzanne is just ten minutes from Cypress Garden and Bok Tower Garden, 40 minutes' drive from Walt Disney World and Epcot, and 45 minutes from Sea World.

CHALET SUZANNE'S BROILED GRAPEFRUIT

1 grapefruit, at room temperature
3 tablespoons butter or butter substitute
1 teaspoon sugar
4 tablespoons cinnamon-sugar mixture (1 part cinnamon to 4 parts sugar)
2 chicken livers (optional)

Slice the grapefruit in half and cut the membrane around center. Cut around each section in each half, close to the membrane, so that the fruit is completely loosened from its shell. Fill the center of each half with 1½ tablespoons butter. Sprinkle ½ teaspoon sugar over each half, then sprinkle each with 2 tablespoons of the cinnamon-sugar mixture. Place the grapefruit on a shallow baking pan and broil just long enough to brown the tops and heat to bubbling hot. Remove from the oven and, if desired, top each grapefruit half with a chicken liver that has been sautéed with flour, salt, and pepper.
SERVES 2.

ℛOYAL SPINACH

2 pounds fresh spinach, washed well, or 2 8-ounce boxes frozen chopped spinach
1 cup boiling salted water
6 tablespoons butter, divided
2 teaspoons Worcestershire sauce
2 teaspoons lime or lemon juice
1 cup sour cream
Salt and freshly ground pepper to taste
1 pound fresh mushrooms, sliced
4 tablespoons dry sherry or chicken broth

Place spinach in one cup of boiling salted water. Cover and cook over low heat until tender. Remove and drain well, then finely chop. Place chopped spinach in a saucepan with 3 tablespoons of butter. Add Worcestershire sauce, lime or lemon juice, sour cream, and salt and pepper to taste. Stir well. In a separate saucepan, melt the remaining 3 tablespoons butter and lightly sauté the sliced mushrooms. Add mushrooms to the spinach mixture. Add dry sherry or chicken broth. Mix together and serve warm.

SERVES 6.

Chef's Note: To serve with your favorite pasta, simply add ½ cup more sour or heavy cream to spinach mixture with salt and pepper to taste.

ℬAKED SHRIMP CURRY

½ cup butter
3 tablespoons all-purpose flour
1 or 2 tablespoons curry powder, to taste
½ tablespoon salt, plus more to taste
¼ teaspoon paprika
¼ teaspoon nutmeg
2 cups half-and-half

3 cups large shrimp, cleaned and cooked
1 tablespoons finely chopped candied ginger or grated fresh ginger
1 tablespoon fresh lemon juice
1 teaspoon onion juice
¼ teaspoon Worcestershire sauce

Preheat the oven to 400°. Melt the butter in a medium nonstick saucepan. Blend in the flour, curry powder, salt, paprika, and nutmeg. Gradually stir in the half-and-half. Cook over medium-high heat until the mixture thickens, stirring constantly. Add the shrimp, ginger, lemon juice, onion juice, and Worcestershire sauce and heat through. Pour into individual 2- to 4-cup baking dishes and bake for 10 minutes or until the tops are lightly browned. Serve over brown or wild rice.

SERVES 4.

Chef's Note: The following condiments may be served on the side: chopped peanuts, chutney, orange marmalade, shredded coconut.

CHALET SUZANNE'S GÂTEAU CHRISTINA

Meringue:
  4 egg whites

1½ cups sugar
⅓ cup blanched ground almonds

Preheat oven to 250°. Cut aluminum foil into 4 8-inch circles and grease each lightly. Whip egg whites until stiff, gradually adding sugar and almonds as eggs begin to stiffen. Place foil rounds on a large baking sheet and spread each evenly with meringue. Bake for 15 minutes or until meringue is dry. Carefully turn meringues over and bake 5 minutes longer.

Chocolate filling:
  2 egg whites
  ¼ cup sugar
  2 tablespoons sweetened cocoa

2 sticks butter, softened
4 ounces semisweet chocolate, melted

In the top of a double boiler, over hot (not boiling) water, beat egg whites until foamy. Gradually add sugar, cocoa, butter, and chocolate, beating until thick and creamy. Remove from heat and cool.

To assemble the gâteau, place the best meringue layer on the bottom and spread with chocolate. Top with another meringue, pressing down lightly to make layers fit together. Spread with chocolate. Repeat until all meringues are used and the top is liberally coated with chocolate. Cover and refrigerate for at least 24 hours.

SERVES 6 TO 8.

$\mathcal{S}$EVEN SISTERS INN

820 S. E. Fort King Street • Ocala, Florida 34471 • (904) 867-1170 • Bonnie Morehardt and Ken Oden

$\mathcal{T}$his grand Victorian was built in 1888 as the residence of the Scott family. A Queen Anne-style beauty, complete with turret, it was restored in 1985 and named the "Best Restoration Project" in the state by the Florida Trust Historic Preservation Society in 1986. In March, 1989, it was chosen "Inn of the Month" by *Country Inns* magazine, and in 1990, it was honored as "one of the twelve best inns in North America."

Each of the seven rooms is decorated to reflect the personality of each of the seven sisters of the Child family, and each room contains a childhood picture, as well as comfortable antiques, teddy bears, and quilts. The Seven Sisters is an ideal spot to catch a glimpse of the past, whether you are sipping raspberry tea on the verandah, strolling the flowering walkways, or playing croquet on the lawn.

Your visit includes a full gourmet breakfast. Creamy baked eggs with caviar, homemade muffins, fresh fruits and juices, French toast stuffed with three kinds of cheese (the recipe included here, it was also featured in *Southern Living* magazine), or baked puffed pancake with glazed fruit and sizzling fresh sausages—the first meal of your day is invariably a taste delight.

Ocala, in Central Florida, is surrounded by green rolling hills and acres of horse farms. You can visit world-famous Silver Springs Park, with its glass-bottom boats, and marvel at the extensive collection in the Appleton Art Museum. The historic downtown, with its quaint town square, includes a variety of antique and gift shops.

$\mathscr{T}$HREE-CHEESE STUFFED FRENCH TOAST

8 slices French bread, 2 inches thick
¾ cup (3 ounces) shredded mozzarella cheese
4 ounces cream cheese, softened
1 tablespoon ricotta cheese
3 tablespoons apricot jam
2 eggs, lightly beaten
½ cup milk
1 cup corn flake crumbs
2 tablespoons butter or margarine
1 12-ounce bottle apricot syrup
¼ cup butter or margarine (½ stick)
2 tablespoons sugar
2 teaspoons ground ginger
16 peach slices
Powdered sugar, sifted

Starting from 1 side, split each bread slice, leaving the opposite side attached (so that it opens like a book). Using a fork, hollow out a shallow pocket on the inside of each slice, discarding crumbs. Set aside. In a small bowl combine the cheeses; stir in the jam. Spoon about 2 tablespoons of the mixture into each bread slice. Put the bread halves together and place in an ungreased 13x9x2-inch baking dish. Cover and refrigerate 8 hours.

Combine the eggs and milk. Dip each piece of bread in the egg-milk mixture, and dredge in corn flake crumbs. In a large skillet over medium heat, melt 2 tablespoons of butter and cook each piece of bread 2 minutes on each side or until golden brown. Place all the bread in a lightly greased 13x9x2-inch baking dish. Bake the French toast at 400° for 15 minutes.

In a saucepan, cook the syrup over low heat until thoroughly heated. Remove from the heat and keep warm.

Combine ¼ cup butter (½ stick), sugar, and ginger in a large skillet over medium heat; add the peaches and cook three minutes, stirring gently. Arrange the French toast on individual plates; top each serving with peach slices and sprinkle with powdered sugar. Serve with warm apricot syrup.

SERVES 8.

Chef's Note: This recipe appeared in *Southern Living* magazine.

GG ENCHILADAS

1½ teaspoons vegetable oil	2 tablespoons milk
1 small onion, chopped	Salt and pepper to taste
½ green pepper, chopped	4 large thin flour tortillas
1 15-ounce can stewed tomatoes	½ cup shredded Cheddar cheese,
1 teaspoon chili powder	divided
4 eggs	

Pour the vegetable oil into a sauté pan and then sauté the onion and green pepper until limp. Add the stewed tomatoes and chili powder and simmer over low heat. Beat the eggs with the milk and salt and pepper.

Dip flour tortillas in tomato-onion mixture until wet. Place on a plate; sprinkle a little of the shredded cheese and spread ¼ of the egg mixture in the center of each tortilla. Roll and place with seam side down in a lightly greased glass dish. Pour remaining sauce over tortillas. Cover with remaining cheese and place under preheated broiler until cheese is melted.

SERVES 4.

CASA DE SOLANA

21 Aviles Street • St. Augustine, Florida 32084 • (904)824-3555 • Faye McMurry

*T*he Don Manuel Solana House (1793) is located on a cobblestone street in the historic district of St. Augustine, America's oldest city. Here the rhythmic clip-clop of horse and buggy never sound dated, and there's history around every corner. Accommodations include four antique-filled guest rooms. You can ask for a fireplace or for a balcony with views overlooking the house's beautiful garden or breath-taking Mantanzas Bay. The enclosed courtyard is lushly tropical and includes a goldfish pond—a splendid place to sip a cup of tea while daydreaming of the past or planning for the days to come.

St. Augustine is located between Jacksonville and Daytona Beach on Florida's eastern coast. The city truly offers something for everyone. St. Augustine's romantic and exciting past has been faithfully preserved, so visitors can wander its narrow, picturesque streets, admire the colonial buildings, and explore the battlements of Fort Castillo de San Marcos. Forty miles of wide, sandy beach beckon sun-lovers, and with Marineland, golf, tennis, and water sports opportunities close at hand, St. Augustine is the complete vacation destination.

AKE-UP CASSEROLE

2 cups seasoned croutons
1 cup shredded Cheddar cheese
1 4-ounce can mushroom pieces, drained
1½ pounds country fresh sausage, browned and crumbled
½ cup chopped onion
6 eggs

2½ cups milk (separated)
½ teaspoon salt
½ teaspoon pepper
½ teaspoon dry mustard
1 10¾-ounce can cream of mushroom soup
½ cup milk

Place croutons in a greased, 13x9x2-inch pan. Top with the cheese and mushrooms. In a skillet brown the sausage and onion; drain and spread over the cheese. In a bowl beat the eggs with 2 cups of the milk and seasonings; pour over the sausage. In a separate bowl mix the soup with ½ cup milk and spread on top. Bake at 325° for 1 hour.

SERVES 8.

Chef's Hint: Allow to cool and slice if you are going to freeze for later use

LOST BREAD (PAIN PERDU)

Chef's Note: This recipe was given to us several years ago by a Sarasota client who had become intensely interested in New Orleans cuisine. Its name "Lost Bread" refers to the fact that it was a way to use stale bread. He said he did not know of any New Orleans restaurant that now serves it. We once saw a reference to "lost bread" in a culinary article on New Orleans, but it was described as French Toast. The real secret of this recipe seems to be that the frying process caramelizes the strawberry preserves. We have tried other kinds of preserves, but none seems to taste as good as strawberry.

2 slices French bread (1½ to 2 inches thick)
Strawberry preserves
2 eggs
2 tablespoons half and half
Dash of vanilla extract
Cooking oil
Powdered sugar

Cut the crust off the bottom side of the bread and then cut a pocket in the bottom. Fill the pocket with a heaping tablespoon of strawberry preserves and press the pocket closed. In a bowl beat together the eggs, half and half, and vanilla. Soak the bread in the egg mixture for a minute or so. In a deep fry pan (we use a Chinese wok) heat enough oil to completely cover the slice of bread so that when you lay the filled slice of bread in it, it will brown quickly. As soon as it is brown, turn it over and brown the other side. Drain on a paper towel and sprinkle with powdered sugar.

SERVES 1.

Chef's Hint: If you are preparing for a large number, keep the bread warm in the oven and sprinkle with sugar just before serving.

$\mathscr{E}$GG STRATA

12 slices French bread with crusts removed, cut into cubes
1½ cups diced ham (approximately ½ pound)
½ bell pepper, diced
½ red pepper, diced
⅓ cup onion, diced or minced
¾ cup grated Cheddar cheese
¾ cup Monterey Jack cheese, grated
9 eggs
1 teaspoon salt
3 teaspoons dry mustard
3 cups milk

Spray an oblong pan (9x13-inch) with cooking oil spray, and place bread on bottom. Combine the ham, peppers, onion, and cheeses and pour over bread. Mix together the eggs, salt, mustard, and milk and pour over. Cover with plastic wrap and let sit in refrigerator overnight. Bake in 350° oven for 1 hour.

SERVES 10 TO 12.

Chef's Note: My guests here at the Casa love it!

$\mathscr{B}$REAKFAST SCONES

2 cups all-purpose flour
3 tablespoons sugar
2 teaspoons baking powder
½ teaspoon baking soda
¼ teaspoon salt
⅓ cup butter or margarine
½ cup sour cream

1 egg, slightly beaten
⅔ cup currants (optional)
2 teaspoons milk
1 tablespoon sugar
Strawberry butter (recipe follows)

Combine flour, sugar, baking powder, soda, and salt, in a medium bowl and stir well. Cut in butter with a pastry blender until mixture forms coarse crumbs. Add the sour cream and the egg, stirring just until dry ingredients are moistened. Stir in currants, if desired.

Turn dough out onto a lightly floured surface and knead lightly 4 to 5 times. Pat dough into an 8-inch circle on a greased baking sheet. Brush top with milk and sprinkle with 1 tablespoon sugar. Cut circle into 8 wedges; using a sharp knife to separate wedges slightly. Bake at 400° for 14 to 16 minutes or until lightly browned. Serve scones with Strawberry Butter.

MAKES 8 SCONES.

$\mathscr{S}$TRAWBERRY BUTTER

½ cup butter, softened

2½ tablespoons strawberry preserves

Cream butter and stir in preserves. Transfer to a small serving bowl.
MAKES ½ CUP.

TOMATO AND SPRING ONION QUICHE

1 9-inch pastry shell
4 strips bacon, cooked crisp
1 cup sliced spring onions
1 green pepper, chopped
1 cup grated Cheddar cheese
5 eggs
¾ cup half-and-half

½ teaspoon salt
¼ teaspoon black pepper
⅛ teaspoon garlic powder
3 or 4 plum tomatoes, sliced
  thick
1 teaspoon Italian seasoning

Preheat oven to 350°. Cook bacon until crisp and drain and crumble. Spread sliced onions over pie crust and top with crumbled bacon, chopped green pepper, and cheese. Put eggs, half-and-half, salt, pepper, and garlic powder in a blender and blend until well mixed. Pour egg mixture over the ingredients in pie crust. Carefully arrange tomato slices on top and sprinkle with Italian seasoning. Bake at 350° for 30 to 40 minutes.

SERVES 6 TO 8.

OLD CITY HOUSE INN & RESTAURANT

115 Cordova Street • St. Augustine, Florida 32084 • (904) 826-0781 • John and Darcy Compton

*I*n the heart of St. Augustine's historic district, this inn, built around 1873, is one of the city's finest examples of Colonial Revival architecture. The house originally served as the stable for the Ammidown Mansion. At times it has been a winter cottage rented to wealthy Northerners, a hat shop, an antique shop, apartments, and recently, an office building. In 1990, it was returned to its original style and colors, but with modern conveniences.

Each guest room has a private entrance, a queen-size bed, cable television, and bath. Smoking is permitted on the verandah and in the courtyard. Your stay includes a bountiful breakfast, as well as complimentary wine and cheese at your arrival or following an afternoon of sightseeing. For a special touch of elegance, you can plan to dine at the Old City House Restaurant, which is recognized as one of Florida's top 100.

Bicycles are available at the inn for leisurely tours of the city, and the inn is within walking distance of the Intercoastal Waterway and the unique shops and historic attractions of the nation's oldest city. St. Augustine's lovely beaches are located six miles away, over the impressive Bridge of Lions.

EGGS DIJON

2 cups sour cream
1 tablespoon Dijon mustard
Salt to taste
¼ cup white wine (a good
   Chardonnay is best)

8 eggs
4 tablespoons grated smoked
   Gouda cheese, grated
   Unseasoned breadcrumbs

Spray 4 ramekins generously with cooking oil spray. In a bowl with a wire whisk, mix together the sour cream, Dijon mustard, a pinch of salt, and the wine. Drop two eggs in each ramekin and cover with the grated cheese. Drop dollops of sour cream mixture over the eggs and top with breadcrumbs. Bake at 350° for 12 to 15 minutes.
SERVES 4.

OLD CITY HOUSE POPPY SEED MUFFINS

2 cups all-purpose flour
¼ cup poppy seeds
½ teaspoon salt
¼ teaspoon baking soda
½ teaspoon baking powder
½ cup butter (1 stick)

¾ cup brown sugar
2 eggs
½ cup buttermilk
1 teaspoon vanilla extract
1 teaspoon lemon juice

Grease a muffin tin. In a medium bowl, combine flour, poppy seeds, salt, baking soda, and baking powder. Using an electric mixer, cream the butter and sugar until thick. Beat in the eggs, 1 at a time. Blend in the buttermilk, vanilla, and juice. Gradually beat into the dry ingredients. Spoon batter into the prepared tin. Bake at 350° about 20 minutes or until tester comes out clean. Cool 5 minutes before removing from the tin.
MAKES 12 MUFFINS.

OLD CITY HOUSE LOW COUNTRY FRIED GRITS

2 cups chicken stock
1 cup heavy cream
2 cups white grits
1 cup fresh shrimp (diced raw)
½ cup diced scallions
½ cup shredded sharp Cheddar cheese

Salt and pepper
All-purpose flour seasoned with salt and pepper
Unsalted butter for frying
Low Country bacon gravy (recipe follows)

In a large saucepan combine the chicken stock with the heavy cream and boil. Add the grits to the boiling mixture and cook for 30 minutes over medium-high heat. Add the shrimp, scallions, and Cheddar cheese and simmer for 10 minutes. Pour mixture into a greased loaf pan and let chill overnight. Slice into ¼-inch rectangles and dredge in flour seasoned with salt and pepper. Pan fry in unsalted butter until golden brown on each side. To cut calories, substitute skim milk thickened with flour for the heavy cream. Top with Low Country Bacon Gravy (recipe follows).

SERVES 8.

$\mathcal{L}$OW COUNTRY BACON GRAVY

1 pound bacon, chopped
1 large yellow onion, chopped
½ cup all-purpose flour
1 quart heavy cream

2 teaspoons Creole spice
1 grilled shrimp, optional, per
serving

In a large skillet, cook the bacon and onion over high heat until the bacon is crisp. Set the cooked bacon aside; do not drain the grease. To the bacon grease add flour and blend well. Add heavy cream and seasoning, stirring constantly until thick. Pour over the fried grits and garnish with 1 grilled shrimp if desired.

MAKES 1½ QUARTS.

$\mathcal{C}$HICKEN CRÊPES

2 tablespoons butter
3 8-ounce chicken breasts, sliced
in thin strips
1 cup onions, cut julienne
1 cup sliced mushrooms

Basil Cream Sauce (recipe
follows)
6 crêpes (available in most
supermarkets)

In large skillet, over medium heat, melt the butter and sauté the chicken breasts until half done. Add the vegetables and cook until chicken is done. Add 1⅓ cups of Basil Cream Sauce and simmer 5 minutes over low heat. Spoon one sixth of the mixture into a crêpe, roll it up and place on a warm plate. Top with a little basil cream to garnish. Repeat steps for balance of ingredients. Serve with sliced fresh fruit.

SERVES 2 TO 3.

BASIL CREAM SAUCE

2 cups heavy cream
3 bouillon cubes, dissolved in ¼ cup boiling water

Roux
½ cup chopped fresh basil

In as saucepan over medium heat, bring cream and bouillon to a simmer and add the roux to thicken. Strain through a fine sieve. Add basil and let stand on low heat. (Can be refrigerated for 1 week).

Chef's Hint: Try adding any of your favorite vegetables to the chicken.

Authors' Tip: To reduce calories, use half and half to replace heavy cream. Fresh fruit such as kiwi, orange rounds, and grapes along with the chicken makes an attractive presentation. Save time by preparing the sauce ahead of time.

Authors' Note: White or brown roux are the most common thickeners for savory sauces. A roux is a mixture of flour and fats blended together gently over very low heat for 5 minutes or longer.

MAKES A LITTLE OVER 2 CUPS.

CASTLE GARDEN

15 Shenandoah Street • St. Augustine, Florida 32084 • (904) 829-3839 • Bruce Kloeckner and Kim VanKooten Kloeckner

The motto of Castle Garden is, "Stay at a Castle and be treated like ROYALTY." The newly renovated 1860s inn is an intriguing example of Moorish Revival style. Its unusual coquina stone exterior remains virtually untouched, and the foundation and chimney from the old Blacksmith's shop still stand. You can relax in a wicker rocker under the portico and enjoy the lush tropical landscaping of the gardens. This is a place for romance and refuge.

The inn includes six guest rooms, all furnished with period antiques. Two Bridal Rooms offer sunken bedrooms, Jacuzzis, cathedral ceilings, and more surprises. You will feel like royalty in your bubble-filled Jacuzzi, by candlelight, with a bottle of complimentary wine or champagne to celebrate. You'll awake to the aroma of freshly baked goodies and enjoy a full country breakfast "just like mom used to make." Other amenities included in your rates are chocolates on your pillow, bicycles for tours of St. Augustine, and private fenced parking. Ask about additional amenity packages such as picnic lunches or horse-and-buggy tours.

$\mathscr{B}$ROCCOLI QUICHE

1 10-ounce package frozen
  broccoli (chopped)
1 deep dish pie shell
1 cup shredded Swiss or
  Monterey Jack cheese
4 teaspoons onion flakes

3 eggs, beaten
1 cup half and half
½ cup milk
½ teaspoon seasoned salt
  Pepper
  Grated Parmesan cheese

Cook the broccoli as directed; drain and cool. Arrange the cheese on the bottom of the pie shell. Add the broccoli and the onion flakes. In a bowl, blend the eggs, half and half, milk, and seasonings. Pour mixture into the pie shell and sprinkle Parmesan cheese on top. Bake at 375° for 40 to 45 minutes. Allow to cool 5 minutes before serving.

Serves 4 to 6.

Chef's Hint: For variation, add crumbled bacon, cut up sausage links, or any cooked breakfast meats.

Authors' Tip: This dish goes well with fresh fruit or hot curried fruits.

$\mathscr{C}$ASTLE GARDEN SOUFFLÉ

6 slices white bread
6 eggs
2 cups milk
1 cup breakfast meat, cooked
  (crumbled bacon, cut up
  sausage links, or diced ham)

1 cup grated Cheddar cheese
  Salt and pepper

Remove crusts from bread and cut the bread into cubes. Beat the 6 eggs, add the milk and stir. Add the cubes of bread. Let soak; beat with mixer; refrigerate overnight. The next morning pour half the bread mixture into the top of a double boiler (egg mixture in the top pan and water in the bottom pan and add all the meat and ¾ of the grated cheese. Pour in the rest of the egg mixture and sprinkle the rest of the grated cheese on top. Bake in an oven 1 hour at 325° or until golden brown.

SERVES 6.

Chef's Hint: Add cooked broccoli, cauliflower, or any kind of cooked vegetable.

OW PATTIES

A Ingredients
- 2 cups sugar
- 3 tablespoons cocoa
- ½ cup butter or margarine (1 stick)
- ½ cup milk

B Ingredients
- 1 teaspoon vanilla extract
- ½ cup peanut butter
- 3 cups instant oatmeal

In a saucepan bring all the ingredients in the A list to a boil. Boil for 1 minute. Remove from heat and add the ingredients from the B list. Stir and drop by spoonfuls onto waxed paper. Let cool. Refrigerate prior to serving.

MAKES 24.

FERNCOURT BED & BREAKFAST

PO Box 758 • San Mateo, Florida 32187 • (904) 329-9755 • Jack and Dee Dee Morgan

*L*ovingly restored, this many-roomed "painted lady" was built in 1889. Today, it features five guest bedrooms, each with private bath, and you can select your choice of queen, king or double beds. Ferncourt is also wheelchair accessible.

You will begin your day with a delicious gourmet breakfast served in the dining room or the breakfast room or on the spacious wraparound verandah. Specialties of the house include light and luscious soufflés, old-fashioned rice pudding, and breakfast cheesecake, as well as tasty baked breads, syrups, jams, jellies, and tangy lemon curd—all products of the Ferncourt kitchen.

Located just 25 miles from historic St. Augustine, San Mateo was a bustling town at the turn of the last century. Today this quiet hamlet offers a convenient base from which to explore the many attractions of North Central Florida. You can also cheer for your favorite driver at the nearby auto races or spend a fun day of shopping and people-watching at a local festival. If angling is your sport, you will find some of the world's best fishing spots virtually at your doorstep.

FERNCOURT RICE PUDDING

4 ounces cream cheese, softened
½ cup sugar
2 eggs
2 teaspoon vanilla extract
2 cups half and half
½ teaspoon salt (optional)
2 cups cooked rice, regular or instant
Nutmeg

Combine the cream cheese with the sugar. Add eggs and beat well. Add vanilla, half-and-half, and salt, if desired. Pour cheese mixture over the rice and put all into a greased 1-quart bowl. Microwave for 3 minutes; check and stir. Continue cooking for another 3 minutes or until spoon comes out "custardy."

If using a regular oven, place the pudding in a water bath at 350° for about 45 minutes. Stir several times during baking. Serve warm sprinkled with nutmeg. Try adding ½ cup raisins to the rice if desired.

SERVES 8.

NOT JUST ANOTHER BLUEBERRY MUFFIN

1½ cups all-purpose flour
¾ cup sugar
2¼ teaspoons baking powder
½ teaspoon salt
2 small eggs
¾ cup half-and-half
6 tablespoons vegetable oil
1 teaspoon vanilla extract
¾ cup fresh or frozen blueberries (if frozen, do not thaw)

In a medium bowl, stir together the flour, sugar, baking powder, and salt. Blend together the eggs, half-and-half, oil, and vanilla. Add this mixture to the flour mixture. Stir until just moistened. Gently fold in the blueberries. Spoon into paper-lined muffin tin until ¾ full. Bake at 450° for 15 to 20 minutes or until top springs back when touched.

Makes 8 large muffins.

REALLY CREAMY SCRAMBLED EGGS

8 eggs
½ cup cold water
1 teaspoon seasoned salt
2 tablespoons margarine

4 ounces cream cheese, softened
⅓ cup heavy cream
Dill weed or minced parsley for garnish

Beat together the eggs with the cold water. Add the seasoned salt. Heat 2 tablespoons of margarine in a skillet and pour in the egg mixture. Keep heat low. Stir gently until the eggs begin to coagulate slightly. Add the softened cream cheese and cook until the cheese is almost melted. Remove from heat and pour in the heavy cream. Stir gently. Serve immediately with a dusting of dill weed or minced parsley, or, as a last resort, pepper.

MAKES 4 LARGE SERVINGS.

Chef's Note: Here are some tricks for preparing superb scrambled eggs: Always use water, never milk. Seasoned salt adds a special flavor to the eggs.

QUICHE ITALIANO

1 9-inch or 10-inch prepared crust, unbaked
1 small onion, finely chopped
4 ounces of mixed Italian cheese (buy ready mixed in package)

4 large eggs
2 cups whipping cream
½ teaspoon seasoned salt
Tabasco sauce to taste

Spread the onion in bottom of the crust. Cover with cheese. Mix together the eggs, whipping cream, salt, and Tabasco and pour egg mixture over all. Bake in a 350° oven for 45 minutes.

Serves 6 to 9.

Chef's Note: This quiche is my favorite. The mixed Italian cheeses make a much milder flavored custard than the usual Swiss. Serve with tomatoes in vinaigrette or sautéed apples.

$\mathcal{G}$LEN-ELLA SPRINGS

Bear Gap Road • Route 3, Box 3304 • Clarkesville, Georgia 30523 • (706) 754-7295 • Barrie and Bobby Aycock

$\mathcal{G}$len-Ella Springs sits on land that was part of a 600-acre grant to the Davidson family made after the Cherokee Indians were removed from northeast Georgia. The inn takes its name from Glen and Ella Davidson who built a three-room residence on the property around 1870. Some fifteen years later, the Davidsons added guest accommodations. In 1986, the inn was purchased by the Aycocks who were attracted "because it was still standing, relatively unscathed and waiting to be resurrected." Today, the inn can be described as elegantly rustic with a romantic "English countryside chintzy" feel. There are 16 guest rooms tastefully decorated with antiques and locally made handcrafts.

Barrie will tell you all about the renovation, and you might ask about the year she spent in Italy, learning about foods, cooking, and her desire to open a restaurant. Barrie believes in using the freshest ingredients available, and she's not averse to experimentation. The recipe we've included for Abaco Islands French Toast was concocted during a visit with friends in the Bahamas—a kitchen experiment that is now a breakfast legend!

Glen-Ella Springs is located in the foothills of the Blue Ridge Parkway and is just five miles from Tallulah State Park. Nearby Dahlonega and other charming villages celebrate America's first gold rush, which began in 1828, and visitors can try their luck panning for gold. The area is also known for its excellent hiking and world-class white water rafting.

*A*BACO ISLANDS FRENCH TOAST WITH ORANGE-PINEAPPLE SAUCE

Chef's Note: One summer we were fortunate to be invited to spend a few days with our friends, Walter and Jo Ann Lampe, on their boat in the Abaco Islands. One morning her sister-in-law and I volunteered to make French Toast. We took some of the fabulous bread the Bahamians make and started playing around with a sauce for it, using what we could find in the pantry and the fridge. What we came up with was legendary! This was about the time of the movie *When Harry Met Sally* and the unanimous response to everyone's first bite was "Yes! Yes! Yes!" Unfortunately, I'm afraid the special ingredient was Bahamian coconut rum which isn't available in the States, but if you get to the Bahamas, buy some, or let me know if you find an acceptable substitute.

Sauce
2-3 medium oranges
 1 cup (or less) orange-pineapple juice
1½ cups sugar
 ½ teaspoon grated orange peel
 1 to 2 tablespoons coconut rum
 2 tablespoons fresh lime juice
 ⅛ teaspoon salt

Toast
 8 thick slices of egg bread for toast
 4 eggs
 2 cups milk or half-and-half
 ⅛ teaspoon salt
 ¼ cup margarine

Prepare the sauce. Peel and section the oranges, letting the excess juice drip into a bowl. Set the orange segments aside. Measure the juice and add enough orange-pineapple juice to make 1½ cups. Place the juice in small saucepan and add sugar, peel, rum, and lime juice. Boil until it forms a syrup, about 10 minutes. Add orange sections. Keep warm.

Prepare the toast. Combine eggs, milk, and salt in shallow pan and soak bread at least 5 minutes. Melt two tablespoons margarine in a heavy nonstick skillet over medium heat. Cook bread until golden brown on each side. If you are unable to find the coconut rum, substitute cream of coconut, which works very well. Top with the sauce.

SERVES 8.

$\mathscr{M}$OLD OF FRESH SALMON OR SHRIMP

1 pound fresh salmon or 2 pounds shrimp
2 cups mayonnaise
¼ cup grated onion
¼ cup lemon juice
2 tablespoons horseradish
¼ to ½ teaspoon salt

1 to 2 teaspoons chopped fresh dill
2 envelopes unflavored gelatin
½ cup water
(½ cup medium picante sauce if using shrimp)

Prepare the salmon. In a small skillet, place the salmon and enough water to cover. Add a few celery leaves, onion, etc., to season water. Poach gently for 5-10 minutes until salmon is cooked through and flakes easily with a fork. Allow to cool. Crumble coarsely, removing any bones.

Prepare the shrimp. Poach shrimp the same way until shells turn pink. Turn off heat and allow to sit a few minutes to continue cooking through. Let cool, peel, devein, and chop coarsely.

Dissolve gelatin in ½ cup water in the top of a double boiler over boiling water. Cool and combine with mayonnaise, onion, lemon juice, horseradish and dill. Add salmon, or shrimp and picante sauce. Add salt to taste. Pour into 1-quart well-oiled mold and chill overnight. Serve with crackers. Recipe can be doubled or tripled.

FOCACCIA

Many thanks to Jacques Pepin for this idea. Our focaccia has been very well received. You can make it easily.

1 1-pound package frozen bread dough
1½ cups onion, peeled and sliced as thin as possible
1 tablespoon thinly sliced garlic
2 teaspoons fresh or 1 teaspoon dried oregano (or rosemary or thyme)

3 tablespoons extra virgin olive oil
2 tablespoons grated Parmesan cheese

Defrost bread overnight in refrigerator. Roll the dough into a circle about 10-12 inches in diameter; place on a cookie sheet that has been well greased with oil or shortening. Combine onion, garlic, herbs, and olive oil. Spread the mixture evenly over the dough. Sprinkle with cheese, and let rise at room temperature for 40 to 50 minutes. Bake in a 400° oven for about 25 minutes until dough is golden brown and the onions are cooked.

Cool, cut into wedges, and serve warm. May be reheated in low oven for a few minutes—be careful not to burn the onions.

MAKES 6 TO 8 SERVINGS.

OAT BRAN SCONES

We serve these for breakfast all the time. They freeze beautifully.

1¾ cups all-purpose flour
1½ teaspoons baking powder
½ teaspoon baking soda
¼ cup sugar
6 tablespoons (4 ounces) unsalted butter, cold, cut into bits

2 tablespoons heavy cream
½ cup buttermilk
⅓ cup All Bran cereal

Topping:
½ cup heavy cream
½ cup sugar

Combine flour, baking powder, soda, and sugar in mixing bowl. Cut in butter until mixture resembles coarse meal. In another bowl, stir together buttermilk, cream, and bran cereal. Combine and mix with a fork until it masses together.

On lightly floured work surface, pat dough into a disk shape and roll into a circle about ¾-inch thick. Cut into rounds with a 2-inch biscuit cutter. Place scones on lightly greased baking sheet. Brush top of scones with heavy cream using a pastry brush, then sprinkle each one with about 1 teaspoon sugar. Bake at 325° for 20 minutes or until firm and lightly browned on top. If you are planning to freeze the scones, remove from oven before they brown; cool and freeze. They can be reheated from the freezer. Heat at 325° for about 20 minutes, or thaw first if desired. They are best served warm with butter and jelly, or of course, with clotted cream.

MAKES 24 SCONES.

Chef's Note: We have always called this recipe "Oat Bran Scones" even though there are no oats in the ingredients.

EY LIME PIE

1 10-inch prepared graham cracker pie crust

3⅓ cups sweetened condensed milk

½ envelope unflavored gelatin

⅔ cup fresh or bottled Key Lime juice

2 large egg whites, stiffly beaten

1 cup heavy cream

¼ cup sugar

Bake the crust and chill while preparing filling. Heat lime juice to boiling, add gelatin and stir to dissolve. Cool to room temperature. Combine sweetened condensed milk with lime juice, fold in egg whites and chill for at least 6 hours. Whip cream with sugar until stiff. Top with whipped cream before serving.

MAKES 8 SERVINGS.

Chef's Note: We use the old-fashioned Ice Box Pie method. Please, don't put green food coloring in it. Key limes are yellow, not green.

Authors' Tip: Turn this delectable pie into a low fat treat by substituting fat-free sweetened condensed milk and light non-dairy creamer for the heavy cream.

THE YORK HOUSE

P. O. Box 126 • Mountain City, Georgia 30562 • (706) 746-2068 or (800) 231-YORK • Joey Barnes and Ben Collins

The York House has been in continuous operation since 1896, making it the oldest B&B in Georgia. Listed on the National Register of Historic Places, the inn offers 13 guest rooms, all with private baths and entrances opening onto wide-railed porches and breezeways. Each room is furnished and decorated with individual charm. You'll enjoy a walk about the five-acre property, shaded by magnificent hemlock and pre-Civil War Norwegian spruce trees.

Situated between Mountain City and Dillard, near the start of the Appalachian Trail, the area offers outdoor enthusiasts a wealth of recreation opportunities. For majestic scenery, try Tallulah Gorge, the oldest and one of the deepest canyons in North America, and Black Rock State Park. Waterfalls abound along some of the best hiking trails in the eastern United States. The inn is just minutes from several ski resorts, and horseback riding is also close by. White-water rafters can choose from six rivers and lakes within a half-hour drive. The antique shops and art galleries of Mountain City, Dillard, and Clayton provide an abundance of shopping.

After all that activity, relax on the verandah and enjoy a chat with Joey or Ben. They can tell you how the inn began as a two-room log cabin catering to travelers during the railroad era. Ask about the movies that were filmed here and about The York House's famous guests who have included Joel Chandler Harris, the creator of the Uncle Remus tales, and Walt Disney.

*Y*ORK HOUSE BLUEBERRY BUCKLE COFFEE CAKE

This best served warm but it is also delicious at room temperature. Our guests love it!

Cake
½ cup butter (1 stick), softened
½ cup sugar
1 egg
2 cups all-purpose flour
2½ teaspoons baking powder
½ teaspoon salt
½ teaspoon baking soda
⅔ cup buttermilk
2 cups blueberries
Topping (recipe follows)

Preheat oven to 375°. In a bowl, cream together the butter and sugar. Mix in the egg. In a separate bowl, stir together flour, baking powder, salt, and baking soda. Add the dry mixture to the creamed mixture alternately with the buttermilk. Gently fold in the blueberries. Spread the batter in a greased and floured 9x9x2-inch pan. Sprinkle the topping on top of the batter and bake for 50 minutes.

Topping
½ cup all-purpose flour
¼ cup white sugar
¼ cup light brown sugar
½ teaspoon cinnamon
¼ cup butter (½ stick), softened

Sift together sugar, flour, and cinnamon. Cut the butter into dry ingredients until the mixture is crumbly and it is ready to sprinkle.
SERVES 8 TO 10.

SWEET POTATO BISCUITS

2 cups self-rising flour
1 cup shortening

1 cup buttered and sweetened
mashed sweet potatoes
1 cup milk

Sift flour into a mixing bowl. Cut in shortening until the consistency of cornmeal. Add the sweet potato mixture to dough, add a bit of milk and lightly toss. Repeat until the dough is soft. Toss on a floured board and knead gently. Roll into ¼ inch thickness and cut into biscuits. Bake on a lightly greased cookie sheet at 450° for 10 to 15 minutes.

MAKES 12 BISCUITS.

THE GENERALS' QUARTERS

924 Fillmore Street • Corinth, Mississippi 38834 • (601) 286-3325 • Luke Doehner and Charlotte Brandt

Built circa 1872, this Victorian house is located in the historic district of Corinth. Now 70 percent restored by its owners, the house offers five guest rooms featuring modern amenities and handsome antique furnishings. A dignitary from Russia was so enchanted by the 140-year-old, solid cherry bed in his suite that he had his photo taken in the bed. He wanted proof for his Russian friends that the inn was real, and not a museum!

A full breakfast is prepared by Chef Luke. Accommodations also include an evening snack. Luke and Charlotte will be happy to arrange activities that suit your tastes—golf, tennis, boating and fishing are all available.

In the northeastern corner of the state, Corinth is a peaceful Southern community with antique shops, museums and antebellum homes. (Take a walking tour.) But during the Civil War, the town and surrounding country saw more military action than any other area in the Confederate West. More than 300,000 troops from both sides left their legacies in the battlefields and cemeteries that attract history buffs today. The Shiloh National Military Park is nearby, as is NASA's Rocket Motor Facility. For a complete change of pace, plan a short drive south to the birthplace of Elvis Presley, in Tupelo.

THE GENERAL'S CHOCOLATE CAKE

1 4-ounce package Baker's
German sweet chocolate
2¾ cups cake flour
2 teaspoons baking powder
½ teaspoon salt
1 cup butter (2 sticks)
1⅔ cups sugar
4 egg yolks, unbeaten

1 teaspoon vanilla extract
1 teaspoon lemon extract
1 cup milk
1 cup finely chopped walnuts
(can substitute filberts or
pecans)
4 egg whites

Melt the chocolate and allow to cool. Sift together flour, baking powder, and the salt. In a large bowl, cream butter with sugar until fluffy. Beat in egg yolks 1 at a time, beating well. Blend in melted chocolate, vanilla, and lemon. Add flour mixture alternately with milk and then add nuts.

Beat egg whites until they form stiff peaks. Using a rubber spatula, fold the egg whites into the batter.

Pour into a well greased and floured 13x9x2-inch pan and bake at 350° for 50 to 55 minutes. Test with a toothpick to be sure it is done.

SERVES 8.

THE GENERAL'S COCONUT TOPPING

½ cup butter
1 cup firmly packed light brown
sugar

1⅓ cups flaked coconut
⅓ cup half-and-half

In a medium saucepan melt the butter and stir in the sugar, coconut, and half-and-half. Mix well and let stand for about 5 minutes. Cover the General's Chocolate Cake after it has cooled for about 20 minutes with this topping and place under a broiler until the frosting is lightly browned and bubbly.

MAKES 1 CUP.

RED CREEK BED & BREAKFAST INN

7416 Red Creek Road • Long Beach, Mississippi 39560 • (601) 452-3080 • Toni Mertz

Sheltered amid eleven acres of magnolias and ancient oaks, Red Creek Inn was built circa 1899 as a "raised" French cottage. The house's 64-foot front porch is a favorite rest and relaxation spot—a place perhaps to sample the home-grown wines made available to guests by arrangement with a local vintner. The house, handsomely furnished with antiques, includes seven bedrooms and six fireplaces. You are also invited to see and pet the thoroughbred horses on the property, though riding is not permitted.

Long Beach is located on the Gulf of Mexico, between New Orleans and Mobile. Within easy drives, you can also visit Biloxi, Gulfport, and Bay St. John. The entire area is a fascinating blend of Old South history and New South excitement, offering antique shops, interesting museums, fine restaurants, excellent golf courses, and casinos. To complete your vacation agenda, you have quick access to 26 miles of sparkling beaches and Gulf water attractions.

*B*IG SHRIMP OMELET

6 eggs
1 tablespoon butter, melted
1 tablespoon finely chopped
  green onion, plus extra for
  topping
1 teaspoon finely chopped
  parsley

⅓ cup butter
¼ pound peeled, cleaned, freshly
  boiled small shrimp
Pepper
Salt
Garlic salt
American cheese (optional)

In a medium bowl, beat the eggs thoroughly and add 1 tablespoon of melted butter and the onions. Add the parsley and mix lightly. In a warmed cast iron skillet combine ⅓ cup butter and the egg mixture. Increase the heat slightly and roll the mixture as it cooks. Turn the omelet, decrease the heat, and continue to cook. As the softness disappears, add the shrimp, pepper, another sprinkle of green onions, and season lightly with salt and garlic salt.
Serves 2.
Chef's Hint: Delicious served with home-grown, sliced tomatoes and freshly baked bread, rolls, and homemade jams.
Authors' Tip: Frozen shrimp may be substituted for the fresh.

*B*AYOU CHICKEN SURPRISE

4 medium chicken breasts
  Cooking oil
½ medium green bell pepper,
  chopped
1 onion, chopped

1 16-ounce package mild pork
  sausage, cooked and crumbled
¼ teaspoon salt
2 cups chicken broth
1 cup Uncle Ben's rice, uncooked

Cut the chicken breasts into bite-size pieces. In a frying pan combine the chicken with the bell pepper and onion. Add the sausage and salt and sauté until golden brown in enough oil to keep from sticking. Add the chicken broth and rice. Cover the pan and cook slowly for 45 minutes.
Serves 8.

$\mathcal{L}$INCOLN LTD. BED & BREAKFAST

P. O. Box 3479 • 2302 Twenty-Third Avenue • Meridian, Mississippi 39303 • (601) 482-5483

$\mathcal{T}$his B&B is a special find. The original front portion of the historic cottage serves as the office for Lincoln Ltd. Mississippi B&B Reservation Service. The private B&B suite in the back of the cottage consists of a large bedroom with fireplace, private bath, and living room attractively decorated with antiques from the Meridian area. The kitchen is off the living room and has all the modern amenities for guests to make their own continental breakfast. The suite has its own private entrance and carport.

Meridian is an interesting city with some unusual attractions such as the Jimmie Rodgers Museum. Known as the Father of Country Music, Jimmie Rodgers was born and reared in the Meridian area. The annual Jimmie Rodgers Memorial Day Festival attracts visitors from all over the country. The Causeyville General Store and gristmill opened in 1895 and is listed on the National Register of Historic Places. Stone-ground cornmeal is produced on the premises and is available for sale. Restoration has begun on the Grand Opera House of Mississippi, the only second-floor Grand Opera House in the South. Nostalgia posters and more than 1,100 playbills found under the floors represent one of the greatest historical finds in theater history. The city's many parks, lakes, and a municipal golf course are available to visitors.

$\mathcal{H}$ARD-BOILED EGGS WITH MORNAY SAUCE

Hard-boiled eggs (2 per person)   Fried ham

Prepare a casserole of hard-boiled eggs. Cut off 1 end of each egg so it will stand. Cut a cross through each egg so sauce can cover it. Place slices of fried ham between the eggs. Pour Mornay Sauce over all (recipe follows).

$\mathcal{M}$ORNAY SAUCE

1 cup milk
4 ounces butter or margarine
  (1 stick)
1½ tablespoons all-purpose flour

1 cup grated sharp Cheddar
  cheese
Dash paprika
Salt and pepper to taste

Combine milk and butter and heat until butter melts. Dissolve the flour in a little water and add to the saucepan. Cook until thickened. Add the Cheddar cheese. Pour over the eggs. A dash of paprika gives it color. Season with salt and pepper to taste.
MAKES 1 CUP.

 $\mathscr{M}$ONMOUTH PLANTATION

36 Melrose • Natchez, Mississippi 39120 • (601) 442-5852 or (800) 828-4531 • Ronnie and Lani Riches

$\mathscr{T}$he Monmouth of today is the result of the dreams of two men, almost two centuries apart. Built circa 1818, the plantation was purchased in 1826 by General John A. Quitman, a governor of Mississippi and U. S. Congressman, for his wife. The second dreamer is Ron Riches, a businessman with a fascination for the history of the antebellum South, who bought and restored Monmouth to its grand style.

Guest rooms and suites are provided in the main house, slave quarters, carriage house, and plantation cottages. Every day begins with a full Southern breakfast. Other amenities include fragrant soaps and creams, luxurious robes, and complimentary hors d'oeuvres, perfect with a freshly mixed mint julep at the end of the day. You can also make reservations for an elegant five-course dinner by candlelight, served Tuesdays through Saturdays.

Listed on the National Register of Historic Places, Monmouth has welcomed many famous guests, including President Bill Clinton during his governorship of Arkansas. The mansion is ideally located for easy exploration of Natchez. The historic city offers many fascinating sights and magnificent antebellum homes, as well as carriage rides, antique and specialty shops, and a variety of fine dining.

CHEF JUANITA'S ALMOND TULIPS WITH WHITE CHOCOLATE MOUSSE CROWNED WITH RASPBERRY SAUCE

Tulips
- 2 egg whites
- ½ cup sugar
- ½ cup sliced blanched almonds
- ½ cup all purpose flour
- ½ cup butter (1 stick), melted
- 1½ teaspoons vanilla
- ¼ teaspoon almond extract
- dash of salt

In a medium bowl, mix all ingredients together and spoon 2 tablespoonsful onto a cookie sheet. Do only 2 at a time. Bake at 350° for 10 to 15 minutes. Remove quickly and lay on the bottom of a glass turned upside down. Overturn a large cup on top of the "tulip" to mold. Allow to sit 5 minutes and remove. Fill with White Chocolate Mousse and top with Raspberry Sauce.
SERVES 20.

White Chocolate Mousse
- 3 boxes white chocolate baking bars
- 2 pints whipping cream
- Vanilla extract

Cut chocolate into small pieces and melt in double boiler over hot water. Whip the cream. When the chocolate has completely melted, mix thoroughly with whipped cream and vanilla extract.

Raspberry Sauce
- 2 10-ounce boxes frozen raspberries, thawed
- 1 teaspoon cornstarch
- 2 tablespoons lemon juice
- 2 tablespoons kirsch
- Mint sprigs for garnish

Purée raspberries in a blender. Force through a sieve. In a saucepan mix the cornstarch with the lemon juice and add to the raspberry mixture. Bring to a boil and cook until slightly thick. Add kirsch. This will keep for weeks in the refrigerator.
MAKES 2 CUPS.
Pour White Chocolate Mousse into tulips and drizzle Raspberry Sauce over the top. Garnish with a fresh sprig of mint.

CHEF JUANITA'S BRIE WITH PECAN PRALINE SAUCE

1 stick (8 tablespoons) butter
1 cup brown sugar, packed
⅛ teaspoon lemon juice
¼ cup milk

¾ cup pecans, sliced or chopped
1 8-inch round of Brie cheese, at
   room temperature

Mix together the butter, brown sugar, lemon juice, and milk and bring to a full boil. Boil until it thickens, approximately 3 to 5 minutes, stirring constantly. Please not that the mixture burns easily. Pour over the Brie cheese. Top with pecans. Elegant!

SERVES 20.

Chef's Note: Serve the Brie surrounded by sliced green apples and red apples.

THE OLIVER-BRITT HOUSE INN

512 Van Buren Avenue • Oxford, Mississippi 38655 • (601) 234-8043 • Glynn Oliver and Mary Ann Britt

The Oliver-Britt House, a renovated 1905 manor house, offers overnight lodging in gracious Southern style. The inn includes five guest rooms, each uniquely decorated with its own special features. One room is elegantly romantic; another offers New Orleans flair and is spacious enough for a family. One room includes a private telephone line and desk, should you have business to conduct during your stay. Other rooms offer handsome antiques and comfortable queen-size sleeping. On Saturdays and Sundays, breakfast is served by Ilean, whose reputation for Southern cuisine is world-renowned.

USA Today has called Oxford a "thriving New South arts mecca." A city where tradition mingles easily with the contemporary, Oxford is the home of the University of Mississippi—"Ole Miss"—and its museums and annual Jazz Reunion. The focal point of activity in town is "The Square," around which visitors can find historic buildings, excellent restaurants, exciting shops and regularly scheduled live performances of jazz and blues.

Visitors from around the world gather annually for the Faulkner Conference, held in honor of Nobel Prize-winning author and Oxford native William Faulkner. Faulkner's home, Rowan Oak, is preserved as it was during his life and is open to visitors. There is also a permanent Faulkner exhibit in the J. D. Library.

ASPARAGUS SOUFFLÉ

4 eggs
1 15½-ounce can asparagus, drained
1 cup grated Cheddar cheese

1 cup mayonnaise
1 10-ounce can cream of mushroom soup

In a mixer, beat everything until well mixed. Pour into a lightly greased casserole or soufflé dish. Bake at 350° for 50 to 60 minutes.

SERVES 6.

Chef's Hint: Any vegetable may be substituted—spinach, broccoli, squash or corn.

FROZEN FRUIT SALAD

1 cup mayonnaise
1 cup sour cream
1 8-ounce container nondairy whipped topping (or 2 cups of whipped cream)

1 29-ounce can fruit cocktail, drained
1 tablespoon lemon juice
1 cup powdered sugar

Mix all together. Pour into pan and freeze. When hard, cover with plastic wrap.

SERVES 8 TO 10.

Authors' Tip: The recipe works well using low-fat mayonnaise and sour cream and a light nondairy whipped topping. The salad is a refreshing side dish for a spicy entrée like Spanish rice.

FRENCH CHOCOLATE CAKE

Cake

6 squares semisweet chocolate
2 egg yolks, well beaten
1 cup buttermilk
½ cup butter (1 stick)
2 cups sifted light brown sugar
3 cups all-purpose flour
1½ teaspoons salt
1½ teaspoons soda
1 cup very strong coffee
2 teaspoons vanilla extract

Cream Filling

6 ounces semisweet chocolate chips
4 ounces evaporated milk
1 egg, beaten

Topping

2 cups whipped cream
Shaved semisweet chocolate

Rum Glaze

½ cup butter (1 stick)
½ cup sugar
½ cup rum

Prepare the cake. Grease 2 9-inch pans. Line pans with waxed paper and flour the pans. Melt 6 squares of semisweet chocolate in a double boiler. Add egg yolks. Slowly stir in buttermilk. Mix well. Cook until thick. Cool. Cream together butter and brown sugar. Sift flour with salt and soda. Add this to the butter mixture with the coffee. Add the chocolate mixture and vanilla. Pour into the prepared pans. Bake at 325° for about 30 minutes.

To make the rum glaze, mix the ingredients in a saucepan and cook over low heat until the sugar is dissolved. Pour evenly over warm cakes and let cakes stand in the pans until cool. Prepare the filling. In a saucepan, mix the chocolate chips and evaporated milk. Stir over low heat until smooth. Do not boil. Add the beaten egg. Mix well and chill. (If sauce is too thin add a beaten egg yolk.)

To assemble, remove cakes from pans and spread a layer of filling between layers and on top. Whip the cream and ice the entire cake. Shave chocolate overtop.

OAK SQUARE PLANTATION

1207 Church Street • Port Gibson, Mississippi 39150 • (601) 437-4350 or (800) 729-0240 •
Mr. and Mrs. William D. Lum

A visit to Oak Square is like being transported onto the set of *Gone with the Wind*. Built in 1850, this historic plantation was the home of a cotton planter in the glory days of the Old South. The Lums have restored it to its original grandeur, and Oak Square is listed on the National Register of Historic Places. The property comprises the Greek Revival main house, two guest houses, carriage house, and quarters. Guest rooms, with modern amenities, are furnished with eighteenth- and nineteenth-century antiques including romantic canopied beds.

Your day begins with a full Southern breakfast, and then we suggest that you take a tour of the mansion and grounds. Your tour, included in your visit, will include the handsome heirloom antiques that fill the home, the ornate millwork on the ceilings, and the spectacular chandeliers. You can feel the full flavor of antebellum life as you mount the massive divided staircase that leads to an unusual minstrel gallery where musicians once played as guests danced the night away.

On the last weekend in March, Oak Square is host to the annual 1800s

Spring Festival—an event that the Southeast Tourism Society has named one of the Top 20 in the region. More than 200 costumed performers recreate the music, dances, and merrymaking of the nineteenth century. Activities include fencing duels, Maypole dances, lawn games, a period fashion show, Civil War reenactments, and carriage rides.

OURDOUGH BREAD

1 cup Sour Dough Starter (recipe follows)
2 cups lukewarm water
2½ cups unsifted all-purpose flour
1 cup milk
3 tablespoons margarine
3 tablespoons sugar

3 teaspoons salt
1 package active dry yeast
¼ cup lukewarm water
9 cups all-purpose flour, divided
1 teaspoon baking soda
Melted butter

Place starter in a bowl. Add 2 cups water alternately with 2½ cups flour, mixing well with a wooden spoon after each addition. Cover with a towel and let stand in a warm place overnight. The next morning scald the milk in a saucepan and add the margarine, sugar, and salt. Cool to lukewarm. Sprinkle the yeast in ¼ cup lukewarm water. Stir to dissolve. Combine yeast with the milk mixture. Add the milk mixture and 2 cups flour to starter mixture, beating with wooden spoon until smooth. Sprinkle baking soda over batter, stirring gently to mix. Cover bowl with a towel, and let rise in warm place until doubled in size.

Stir down batter gradually. Stir in enough remaining 4½ cups flour to make a dough that leaves the side of the bowl. Knead 5 minutes on a floured board. Divide dough in half and let rise 10 minutes. Shape each half into a loaf. Put in greased loaf pans. Brush with melted butter. Let rise until dough reaches top of pan, about 1 hour. Bake at 375° until done.

MAKES 2 LOAVES.

OURDOUGH STARTER

2 packages active dry yeast
4 cups lukewarm water

4 cups unsifted all-purpose flour

Place the yeast in a glass, stoneware, or plastic bowl. Add ½ cup luke-warm water and stir to dissolve. Add remaining water alternating with flour. Mix well after each addition. Cover with towel in a warm place and let stand at least 6 hours. It will look bubbly and a clear fluid will rise to the top.

Stir before measuring needed amount. After removing needed amount of dough starter, pour remaining mixture into a plastic container. Cover loosely and refrigerate. Starter can be stored in refrigerator indefinately. Replenish starter at least once a week by stirring in ½ cup warm water and ½ cup flour. Cover and let stand at room temperature overnight. The next morning stir down mixture, cover, and refrigerate. This may be used in recipes calling for sour dough starter.

WEET POTATO PONE

4 medium sweet potatoes
½ cup (1 stick) margarine
1½ cups sugar
2 eggs (lightly beaten)
2 tablespoons vanilla extract
2 tablespoons almond extract

2 tablespoons cornstarch
¼ cup milk
2 teaspoons lemon juice (or ¼ teaspoon lemon extract)
Cinnamon to taste

Peel, slice, and boil sweet potatoes until soft. Drain and mash potatoes until they are smooth. Stir in margarine until melted. Add sugar, eggs, vanilla, almond, cornstarch, milk, lemon juice, and cinnamon and stir until well blended. Bake in a lightly greased uncovered baking dish at 350° for 45 minutes to 1 hour for deep dish (about 15 minutes less if using shallow dish).

For sweet potato pie, pour the mixture into an unbaked pastry pie shell and bake at 350° for about 30 minutes. Delicious hot or chilled.

SERVES 12 OR MORE.

Chef's Note: *Pone* is an old Southern term that has been used in cooking since the early nineteenth century. This pone recipe is for a pie that is made without the pie crust, a family recipe and tradition at Oak Sqaure.

FLINT STREET INNS

100 & 116 Flint Street • Asheville, North Carolina 28801 • (704) 253-6723 • Rick, Lynne, and Marion Vogel

The Flint Street Inns are two side-by-side family homes located in the Montford Historic District, Asheville's oldest neighborhood. Opened in 1982, the inns were the first of their kind in Asheville. The homes and furnishings reflect the early twentieth-century style of the area and a time when gracious hospitality was an innate part of family life. Your stay includes a hearty full breakfast served in the dining room.

The inns are within comfortable walking distance of downtown Asheville where you will find a variety of antique and crafts shops and excellent restaurants. While in Asheville, you'll want to visit the nearby Biltmore House and Gardens. The dream-home-come-true of George W. Vanderbilt, the 250-room, Renaissance-style chateau was completed in 1895. Now open to the public, this magnificent 8,000-acre estate includes its own winery. Two sites of literary significance are the Thomas Wolfe Memorial in Asheville and the Carl Sandburg Home in Flat Rock. For nature at its best, the Great Smoky Mountains National Park is practically at your doorstep.

FRENCH TOAST QUEBEÇOISE

8 eggs
1 cup light cream
½ cup brown sugar
4 tablespoons orange juice
4 teaspoons vanilla
Grated peel of one orange
¼ teaspoon nutmeg

¼ teaspoon cinnamon
2 loaves of whole-wheat bread, sliced thick
1 cup butter (2 sticks, ½ stick per four slices of bread)
Powdered sugar for dusting

Mix the first 8 ingredients together. Dip bread in the mixture. In a skillet, melt the butter and fry the bread until golden brown. Sprinkle both sides of the bread with cinnamon while cooking. Before serving, sprinkle with powdered sugar.

SERVES 8.

Chef's Hint: Serve with a garnish of fresh fruit and Apple Cheese Sausage Balls (recipe follows).

Chef's Note: This recipe was found in a B&B trade paper and is available compliments of the Fitch Hill Inn.

APPLE CHEESE SAUSAGE BALLS

2 pounds bulk sausage
8 ounces grated sharp Cheddar cheese
1 egg
1 package unseasoned bread crumbs (or make your own using 4 slices of toasted bread)

4 small apples cored and cut into bite-size pieces (unpeeled)

Mix all ingredients in a large bowl. Using an ice cream scoop as a measure, form into 2-inch balls. Place on greased baking sheet and bake at 300° until done, about 30 to 45 minutes.

MAKES ABOUT 24 BALLS.

Chef's Note: This recipe can be prepared ahead and frozen. Place the baked sausage balls on a pan and partially freeze. Place in freezer bag and use as needed.

*B*EST OVEN CRISP BACON

Use market-style or thick-sliced bacon. Lay the bacon out on a cookie sheet and slowly bake at 250°. When golden brown remove from the oven and drain on paper towels. Reheat to serve.

Chef's Hint: For an interesting variation, dredge the bacon in flour or cornmeal and bake as above.

*M*UFFIN BISCUITS

4 cups self-rising all-purpose flour (can also use Jiffy or other baking mix)
6 tablespoons shortening (if not using Jiffy mix)

1½ cups milk
¼ cup sour cream or whipping cream
½ cup melted butter

Place flour in a large mixing bowl and cut in shortening until crumb stage. Gradually add milk and cream until flour is very moist. Generously grease or spray muffin tin. Using an ice cream scoop as your measure, fill muffin tins.

Bake at 400°. After 5 minutes remove biscuits from oven and brush with melted butter. Return to oven and continue baking until done, approximately 10 to 12 minutes.

Chef's Hint: For an interesting variation, add 1 cup chopped pecans to batter. Also use a combination of honey and melted butter to brush on biscuits.

MAKES 16 BISCUITS.

THE INN AT RAGGED GARDENS

P. O. Box 1927 • Blowing Rock, North Carolina 28605 • (704) 295-9703 • Lee and Jama Hyett

This grand old turn-of-the-century house sits in an attractive garden filled with roses, rhododendrons, and sheltering trees. Originally built as a summer home, the house offers seven charming bedrooms for overnight guests.

Your visit includes a full breakfast served in the dining room or, when the weather is right, in the sun-sparkled walled garden. Three of the recipes we've included come from the kitchen of the former owner, Joseph Villani, a well-known restaurateur and specialist in French and Italian cuisines. Mama's Apple Fritters was a dessert favorite of Villani's mother, Anna, and Kylie's Toast was devised for the Villanis' granddaughter.

Located adjacent to the beautiful Blue Ridge Parkway, Ragged Gardens is literally surrounded by recreation opportunities. For a taste of city life, you are within a comfortable drive of both Asheville and Winston-Salem.

$\mathcal{I}$TALIAN OMELET

2 tablespoons butter
12 eggs
2 tablespoons grated Parmesan
  cheese

3 leaves basil, finely chopped
Chopped parsley for garnish

Melt butter in a sauté pan. Whip together the eggs, Parmesan cheese, and basil leaves. Add the egg mixture to the pan. Flip when lightly brown and repeat on other side. Serve with chopped parsley.

SERVES 6.

Chef's Note: Chef Joe Villani adores Parmesan cheese. His family comes from Parma, Italy, so to Joe, "What's an omelet without Parmesan cheese?"

$\mathcal{M}$AMA'S APPLE FRITTERS

2 large unpeeled Granny Smith
  apples, cubed
1 cup milk
1 cup all-purpose flour
2 eggs

1 teaspoon baking powder
¾ cup cooking oil
1 tablespoon butter or oil
Powdered sugar

Thoroughly mix together the first four ingredients. In a sauté pan, heat the oil and butter until hot. Add tablespoonsful of batter and fry until crispy on both sides. Remove and place on paper towel to remove excess oil. Sprinkle with powdered sugar before serving.

SERVES 6.

Chef's Note: This is former owner Joseph Villani's mother, Anna Villani's recipe. She served it for dessert to her family. Joe likes to serve it to his breakfast guests—and the guests are delighted he does.

Authors' Tip: After frying, pat fritters with paper towels to reduce oiliness.

YLIE'S TOAST

4 ounces cream cheese	2 tablespoons vanilla
12 slices white bread	1 tablespoon cinnamon
2 eggs	Butter
2 cups milk	Powdered sugar

Leave the cream cheese out of the refrigerator until it is spreadable. Spread the bread with the cream cheese and sandwich 2 slices together. Whip together the eggs, milk, vanilla, and cinnamon. Dip 1 sandwich at a time into the egg-and-milk mixture, draining off excess. Cook in a sauté pan in melted butter. Flip the bread over when browned on one side and repeat on other side. Shake powdered sugar on top before serving.

SERVES 6.

Chef's Hint: Freeze the bread before spreading to avoid ripping sandwiches. May be stored frozen. Remove 30 minutes before cooking.

Variations: Add strawberry syrup to the softened cream cheese—or add cinnamon and nutmeg to cream cheese before spreading.

Chef's Note: This recipe was devised by the former owners' daughter for their granddaughter Kylie, because Kylie loves breakfast.

THE HOMEPLACE BED & BREAKFAST

5901 Sardis Road • Charlotte, North Carolina 28270 • (704) 365-1936 • Peggy and Frank Dearien

*B*e prepared to experience the warm and welcoming atmosphere that the name of this B&B promises. Situated on an acre and a half of woodland in southeast Charlotte, The Homestead offers a peaceful oasis amid the bustle of one of the South's fastest growing areas. Ask the Deariens to tell you about the history of the house, which was built in 1902 for a Presbyterian minister, his wife, and seven children.

A delightful Country Victorian, the house includes guest rooms with ten-foot ceilings and heart of pine flooring. The country decor is enhanced by many special touches including quilts and fine linens, handmade accessories, family antiques and original primitive paintings by Peggy's grandfather John Gentry (1898-1989). Your breakfast is just as friendly as your accommodations, and can include such delectables as homemade buttermilk pancakes with fresh blueberry or peach syrup, crepes filled with dilled eggs and topped with a cheese sauce, or chilled poached pears with raspberry sauce.

Although The Homestead may seem like a world unto itself, it is convenient to restaurants and shopping malls and just 15 minutes from uptown

Charlotte. If you love to shop, the local antique stores are a treasure hunter's delight. You will also want to look for bargains at the furniture and textile outlets located a short drive away.

$\mathscr{E}$ASY DILLED EGGS WITH CHEESE SAUCE

1 crêpe
1 egg
1 teaspoon cottage cheese
Salt and pepper to taste

Pinch of fresh dill, crumbled
Dash celery salt
Cheese sauce (recipe follows)

If frozen, remove crêpe from freezer and let thaw at room temperature. Beat together the egg, cottage cheese, salt, pepper, dill, and celery salt. Scramble mixture over medium heat until set. Place egg on crêpe, roll up and set aside. Make cheese sauce.

Cheese Sauce
2 tablespoons instant blending flour
1 cup milk

2 tablespoons butter or margarine
$\frac{1}{8}$ teaspoon salt
$\frac{1}{4}$ cup processed cheese chunks or shredded Cheddar cheese

Blend flour into milk in top of a double boiler. Add butter and salt. Bring water in bottom pan to a boil. Stir mixture over water until thick. Stir in cheese until melted. Remove from heat and let stand over hot water while finishing .

Heat filled crêpe in microwave oven, 20 to 30 seconds per crêpe, until hot. Place on serving plate. Pour sauce over top. Garnish with a slice of hot, cooked bacon and an asparagus spear. Serve at once. This recipe is based on a one crêpe serving. Multiply each ingredient by the number of people to be served.

$\mathscr{P}$EGGY'S BREAD STICKS

2¼ cups self-rising flour
1 tablespoon sugar
¾ to 1 cup milk
1 stick of real butter

Poppy seeds, sesame seeds, Parmesan cheese or any seasoning

Mix together the flour, sugar, and milk to form a dough.

Melt butter in a 9x11-inch pan. Roll out the dough into the size of the pan. Cut down the middle lengthwise—then cut crosswise into strips. Dip the top of each strip into the melted butter and flip over and lay into the melted butter at one end of the pan. After dipping all pieces in the melted butter, add the seeds or toppings. Bake at 450° for 15 to 20 minutes. Serve hot, or cold as a snack.

MAKES 12 TO 16.

Chef's Hint: If using regular flour: add 3¼ teaspoons baking powder, and 1½ teaspoons salt.

$\mathscr{P}$EGGY'S BISCUITS

4 cups self-rising flour
⅔ cup shortening or margarine

2 cups buttermilk (approximately).

Cut a third of the shortening into flour, then the other third. The dough should be a little on the soft and sticky side. Flour the board well.

Chef's Hint: The night before you want to serve the biscuits for breakfast, cut the shortening into the flour with a pastry blender, cover, and let sit overnight at room temperature. In the morning, add the buttermilk and knead just a few times until no longer sticky, then pat or roll out and cut. Bake at 450 for 10 minutes.

MAKES 30 BISCUITS.

Chef's Note: This is a double recipe. It makes a full cookie sheet of biscuits. They freeze well. To reheat, wrap a single layer in foil and heat at 400° for 10 to 15 minutes.

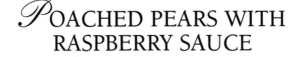OACHED PEARS WITH RASPBERRY SAUCE

4 Bartlett or other green pears,
  halved and cored
  Orange juice

1 stick cinnamon
  Raspberry sauce (recipe
  follows)

Place cored pear halves, cut side up, in bottom of a Dutch oven. Add enough orange juice to cover. Add cinnamon stick. Bring to a boil over medium heat, cover pan, reduce heat to simmer, and cook 10 minutes, or until tender, yet still firm.

Remove pan from heat. Cool pears in liquid. Refrigerate in juice until chilled. Will keep up to one week. Just before serving, make sauce.

SERVERS 8.

RASPBERRY SAUCE

1 cup fresh or frozen raspberries
⅓ cup powdered sugar

¼ cup orange juice, or to taste

Place raspberries in a blender, along with sugar and juice. Process until smooth. Strain and discard seeds. To serve, place each pear half on a dessert plate. Cut pear half from large end toward stem end, being careful not to cut all the way through. Slices should be about ¼ inch thick. Spread into fan shape. Drizzle raspberry sauce across center of each pear half. Garnish with a mint leaf, if desired.

SERVES 8.

THE INN ON PROVIDENCE

6700 Providence Road • Charlotte, North Carolina 28226 • (704) 366-6700 • Darlene and Dan McNeill

This three-story Southern homestead inn is renowned for its warm welcomes and gracious hospitality. The house features five antique- and quilt-filled guest rooms, each with its unique personality. Wind down in a comfortable white wicker chair on the screened-in verandah. Enjoy breeze of the paddle fans and soak in the spectacular view of rolling lawn, garden, tall cedars, and crystalline swimming pool. This is a place to savor the simple pleasures!

Your stay at the inn includes a delicious Southern breakfast served on the verandah when the weather's right. Try the homemade muffins, jams, preserves, and special blend of coffee. Many mornings, Darlene creates her delicious Norwegian heart-shaped waffles served with berries.

*S*AUSAGE BREAKFAST CASSEROLE

1 pound bulk sausage
7 to 8 slices bread, crusts removed,
    buttered and cubed
2 cups shredded sharp
    Cheddar cheese

7 to 8 eggs
2½ cups milk
1 teaspoon salt
1 teaspoon dry mustard

Cook sausage until done, stirring till crumbled. Drain well and pat dry with paper towels. Place buttered bread cubes in a 3-quart casserole. Top with sausage and cheese. Mix remaining ingredients and beat well. Pour over mixture in baking dish and chill at least 8 to 12 hours. Bake at 350° for 40 to 45 minutes.

SERVES 12.

Authors' Tip: For a lovely presentation, serve the casserole with honeydew and cantaloupe slices and a strawberry.

*O*VEN PANCAKE (OR *PANNEKOEKEN*)

½ cup all-purpose flour
½ cup milk
2 eggs, slightly beaten
¼ teaspoon salt
    Pinch nutmeg
1 cup fruit (blueberries, chopped
    apples, etc.)

4 tablespoons butter
    Powdered sugar
    Maple syrup, jam, jelly, or
    marmalade for topping

Preheat oven to 450°. Blend together first 5 ingredients. Beat lightly. Fold in fruit, if desired. Melt butter in a 12-inch ovenproof skillet. When butter is very hot, pour in the batter. Bake 15 minutes or until golden brown. Sprinkle generously with powdered sugar and serve immediately from the skillet with maple syrup, jam, jelly, or marmalade. Doubles nicely.

SERVES 2.

SAUSAGE AND APRICOT TOPPED FRENCH TOAST

1 pound sausage links
1 can (30 ounces) apricot halves, drained
3 tablespoons firmly packed light brown sugar
6 eggs
½ cup biscuit mix

2 tablespoons sugar
½ teaspoon cinnamon
1½ cups milk
1 loaf day-old French bread
Oil
Sour cream

Brown sausage links on all sides, and then push to side of pan. Discard all but 2 tablespoons of drippings. To the drippings add apricots and brown sugar and stir just until sugar dissolves. Mix with sausages and keep warm while making French toast.

In a blender, beat together eggs, baking mix, sugar, cinnamon, and milk. Mix until smooth. Cut bread into 1-inch-thick slices. Soak slices in batter, turning once, till saturated.

In a skillet over medium heat, add about ¼ inch oil. When oil is hot, add a few bread slices at a time. Cover and cook for 5 minutes or until browned and slightly puffy. Turn and do other side. Drain on paper towel and keep warm while doing others. Serve with glazed apricots around French toast. Top with sour cream. Delicious!

SERVES 4 TO 6.

ℬANANA MUFFINS

½ cup butter
½ cup sugar
1 egg
1 cup mashed bananas
1 teaspoon baking soda dissolved
   in 1 tablespoon hot water.

1½ cups all purpose flour
¼ teaspoon salt
1 teaspoon nutmeg
½ cup walnuts, chopped

Using an electric mixer, cream the butter and sugar. Add the egg, bananas, and baking soda, combining well. Blend in the flour, salt, nutmeg, and nuts. Bake in greased muffin tins at 375° for 20 minutes.

MAKES 12 MUFFINS.

Chef's Hint: Simple and very good. For variation add coconut or chocolate chips.

ℂURRIED FRUIT COMPOTE

½ cup butter or margarine
   (1 stick)
1 tablespoon cornstarch
1 teaspoon curry powder
¾ cup brown sugar
1 can chunk pineapple, drained

1 can sliced pears, drained
1 can sliced peaches, drained
1 small jar sliced candied apples,
   cut in halves, drained
A handful of raisins

In a saucepan melt the butter. Add cornstarch, curry powder, and brown sugar and heat through. Mix fruit in a buttered casserole dish. Pour hot sugar mixture overtop. Mix and bake in a 350° oven for 30 minutes until piping hot.

SERVES 8 TO 10.

ARROWHEAD INN

106 Mason Road • Durham, North Carolina 27712-9201 • (919) 477-8430 • Barbara B. Ryan

*O*riginally the center of a 2,000-acre plantation, the main part of this history-steeped manor house was built circa 1775 and has been expanded several times over the past two centuries. The property faces a road that was part of the Great Trading Path used for centuries by coastal and mountain Indians. The path stretched from Bermuda Hundred on the James River in Virginia to the Smoky Mountains, and people who live along the trail today can still find artifacts attesting to the history of the Native Americans who once traveled this way.

The Ryans furnished the inn with respect for its fascinating past—from rustic Early American to nineteenth-century "High Style." Many of the furnishings, quilts, china, and other decorative pieces come from the Durham area because, says Barbara, "We are big believers in 'sense of place' as a travel enhancement."

Breakfast is served in the formal dining room or the beamed and brick-floored Keeping Room or, when the weather permits, on the brick patio beneath 150-year-old-magnolias. We recommend you sample the homemade fig, quince and crab apple preserves. And who knows who might join you for breakfast? Former guests have included entertainers Dudley Moore, Emmy Lou Harris, and Loudon Wainwright.

SCRAMBLED EGGS AU GRATIN

6 tablespoons margarine
6 tablespoons all-purpose flour
3 cups milk
½ teaspoon salt
½ teaspoon pepper
½ pound mushrooms, sliced

¼ cup vermouth or lemon juice
12 eggs
½ cup milk
2 tablespoons butter
½ pound cooked, crumbled bacon
½ pound grated Cheddar cheese

In a large skillet, melt the 6 tablespoons margarine and blend in flour until smooth. Slowly add 3 cups milk and simmer until thick and smooth. Add salt and pepper. In a separate skillet, sauté mushrooms in vermouth or juice. Blend mushrooms into thickened milk. Beat eggs in the ½ cup milk. Melt butter and pour into the eggs, stirring over medium heat until tender. Combine the eggs with the milk-and-mushroom mixture. Stir in bacon and cheddar cheese. Pour mixture into a greased, large, shallow casserole. Bake at 325° for 30 minutes.

SERVES 10 TO 12.

Chef's Hint: The recipe may be prepared a day ahead. Bring to room temperature before baking.

ASPARAGUS TOMATO QUICHE

4 beaten eggs
3 tablespoons all-purpose flour
1 teaspoon salt
½ teaspoon dry mustard
1 teaspoon paprika
1½ cups light cream

2 cups Swiss cheese, grated
10 fresh asparagus spears washed and trimmed
1 10-inch pie shell, lightly baked
1 tomato sliced in four slices

Preheat oven to 375°. Beat eggs, flour, salt, mustard, paprika, and light cream. Add cheese. Set aside 6 asparagus spears for the top; chop the remainder into 1-inch pieces. Place them on the bottom of the pie shell, and pour the egg mixture over them. Bake about 20 minutes. Remove from oven and quickly arrange tomato and remaining asparagus on top in a pleasing pattern. Return to the oven for about 15 to 20 minutes. Cut into portions and serve.

SERVES 4 TO 6.

$\mathscr{F}$RENCH TOAST LORRAINE

1⅔ cups milk
2 eggs
½ cup grated Parmesan cheese
1 teaspoon prepared mustard

8 slices French bread, cut 1-inch thick
4 slices bacon, cooked and crumbled

Combine milk, eggs, cheese, and mustard and soak the bread slices in it overnight. Sauté the bread slices. Serve on a warmed plate with the bacon sprinkled on top.

SERVES 4.

Chef's Hint: Great with maple syrup.

$\mathscr{S}$PICED POPOVERS WITH CRAN-ORANGE SPREAD

3 eggs, slightly beaten
1 cup all-purpose flour
1 tablespoon sugar
1 teaspoon apple pie spice

¼ teaspoon salt
1 cup milk
3 tablespoons melted butter

Combine all ingredients in a blender or food processor until smooth. Grease muffin pans. Preheat pans. Fill each cup half full. Bake 15 minutes at 425°. Reduce heat to 350° and bake popovers 12 to 15 minutes more until firm to the touch. Serve immediately with accompanying spread.

MAKES 12 POPOVERS.

CRAN-ORANGE SPREAD

1 3-ounce package cream cheese
3 tablespoons cranberry-orange
   sauce (recipe follows)

½ teaspoon orange extract

Beat cream cheese until smooth and blend in sauce and extract.
MAKES ½ CUP.

CRANBERRY ORANGE SAUCE

¾ cup white sugar
¾ cup orange juice
½ stick cinnamon

3 cups fresh or frozen cranberries
   Grated rind of 1 orange

Bring to a boil the sugar, orange juice, and cinnamon stick. Reduce heat
and simmer for 3 minutes. Add cranberries and orange peel and cook 10 minutes more. Allow to cool. Remove cinnamon stick. Extra sauce may be stored
in the refrigerator.
SERVES 6.

FRESH FRUIT KABOB

½ cup rum
   Juice of an orange
   Juice of ½ lemon
   Grated cinnamon stick
2 tablespoons honey

1 pineapple
3 kiwi
3 bananas
1 pint strawberries

Mix rum, juices, and honey with a pinch of cinnamon. Cut the pineapple
into cubes. Quarter the kiwi and cube the bananas. Hull the strawberries.
Skewer the fruit alternately. Brush with the syrup and broil them lightly, bast-
ing with the syrup. Serve immediately.
SERVES 6.

BUTTONWOOD INN

190 Georgia Road • Franklin, North Carolina 28734 • (704) 369-8985 • Liz Oehser

This small and cozy country inn is a delight for people who enjoy simplicity and the rustic beauty of Mother Nature. Dogwood and rhododendron present a spectacular display every spring, and fall's foliage is brilliant. Nestled among tall pines, the inn is delightfully furnished in country home style with antiques, handmade family quilts, collectibles, and country crafts.

Each morning begins with a full breakfast, and dishes range from country to gourmet. Culinary treats may include puffy scrambled eggs, souffles, apple sausage rings, baked peaches and sausage, or stuffed French toast. Liz says she is addicted to cookbooks: "They are my trashy novels! I get more enjoyment out of recipes than I do reading a paperback."

Buttonwood Inn is located just a short distance from the Smoky Mountain and Blue Ridge Parkways. The area offers an abundance of activities including gem mining, white water rafting, horseback riding, and hiking, as well as excellent crafts shopping and restaurants.

STRAWBERRY OMELET WITH STRAWBERRY BUTTER

3 eggs (separated), whites at
  room temperature
3 tablespoons sugar (separated)

1 tablespoon rum
Pinch salt

Butter a 10-inch oven-proof skillet or omelet pan. Preheat oven to 350°. Beat together the yolks, 2 tablespoons sugar, and rum. Add pinch of salt to egg whites and beat until frothy. Gradually add 2 tablespoons sugar and beat till peaks form.

Fold into yolks. Bake for 20 minutes. Top with strawberry butter (recipe follows).

SERVES 2.

STRAWBERRY BUTTER

Whip ½ cup unsalted butter (1 stick). Add ½ cup strawberry jam and 1 teaspoon lemon juice. Whip till smooth. Refrigerate. Spread butter on half of omelet and fold over. Top with 2 tablespoons strawberry butter, 2 tablespoons sour cream, and 2 sliced strawberries.

BLINTZ SOUFFLÉ

Filling
1 16-ounce carton (2 cups) small
  curd cottage cheese
2 egg yolks
1 tablespoon sugar
1 teaspoon vanilla extract
8 ounce cream cheese, softened

Batter
1 cup all-purpose flour
1½ cups sour cream
½ cup orange juice
6 eggs
¼ cup margarine, softened
⅓ cup sugar
2 teaspoons baking powder
½ teaspoon cinnamon
Sour cream and fruit preserves
for topping

Grease a 13x9-inch pan. Beat together all the filling ingredients and set aside. Spoon flour in cup and level off. In blender, place sour cream, orange juice, eggs, margarine, flour, sugar, baking powder, and cinnamon. Cover and blend till smooth, scraping sides often. Pour half of batter into pan. Drop filling by teaspoons over batter. (Filling will mix slightly with batter). Pour remaining batter over filling. Cover and refrigerate at least 2 hours or overnight. Bake at 350° for 50 to 60 minutes till puffy and brown. Top with sour cream and warm preserves.

SERVES 12.

ℴVERNIGHT ORANGE FRENCH TOAST

4 eggs	1 teaspoon vanilla extract
⅔ cup orange juice	12 slices thick-cut French Bread
⅓ cup milk	½ butter
¼ cup sugar	½ cup nuts
¼ teaspoon nutmeg	

Beat eggs with wire wisk. Beat in orange juice, milk, sugar, nutmeg, and vanilla. Cut and place thick slices of French bread in 13x9x2-inch dish. Pour mix over bread and turn pieces to coat. Cover and refrigerate overnight.

Melt ½ cup butter in jellyroll pan. Spread evenly and arrange bread in single layer. Spread ½ cup of nuts on bread. Bake at 375° for 20 to 25 minutes till puffy and brown.

SERVES 6 TO 8.

Chef's Hint: Great with our Baked Peaches and Sausage.

STUFFED FRENCH TOAST

16 slices French bread
Filling
  8 ounces cream cheese, softened
1½ teaspoons vanilla extract,
    divided
  ½ cup chopped nuts
  4 eggs

½ teaspoon nutmeg
1 cup whipping cream
  Powdered sugar
Topping
1 12-ounce jar apricot jam
½ cup orange juice

Cut bread into 1-inch slices and cut slits in the sides of the bread slices to make pockets. Combine cream cheese, 1 teaspoon vanilla, and nuts. Fill each pocket with 1 tablespoon of the filling.

In a large bowl, beat together the eggs, ½ teaspoon vanilla, nutmeg, and whipping cream. Dip the bread into the egg mixture and cook in a greased skillet over medium-high heat until lightly brown on both sides. Sprinkle with powdered sugar. Combine apricot jam and orange juice and use as topping for French toast.

SERVES 8.

SAUSAGE RING

2 pounds sausage (half hot and
    half mild)
1½ cups cracker crumbs
  2 eggs beaten

½ cup milk
¼ cup chopped onions
1 cup chopped apples
16 eggs, scrambled

Mix all the ingredients together except the eggs and place in a greased ring mold. Bake at 350° for one hour. When done, unmold and fill the center of the ring with scrambled eggs. The recipe makes 2 rings and may easily be halved.

ONE RING SERVES 8.

Chef's Hint: The sausage ring may be baked for 30 minutes and frozen. Bake an additional 30 minutes when ready to serve.

BAKED PEACHES AND SAUSAGE

1 pound sausage
1 29-ounce can peach halves
¼ cup brown sugar
½ teaspoon cinnamon
¼ teaspoon ground cloves

Cook and drain sausage. Press out excess grease. Drain peaches and reserve ¼ cup juice. Place peaches cut side up in greased 10x6x2-inch dish and add reserved juice. Combine brown sugar, cinnamon, and cloves and sprinkle over peaches. Bake 15 minutes at 425°. Add the sausage and bake an additional 15 minutes.

SERVES 6.

COFFEE BRAN MUFFINS

¾ cups all-purpose flour
2 teaspoons baking powder
½ teaspoon salt
½ teaspoon cinnamon
1 cup unprocessed bran
½ cup (cold) coffee
1 tablespoon margarine, melted
½ cup sugar
1 egg, beaten
½ cup raisins/currants

Sift together first four ingredients. Stir in bran. Combine and blend together the coffee, margarine, sugar, and egg. Gradually pour liquid into dry ingredients. Fold in raisins. Pour into greased muffin tin and bake 15 minutes at 400°.

MAKES 8 MUFFINS.

LEMON MUFFINS

1 cup margarine or shortening
1 cup sugar
4 egg yolks
½ cup lemon juice
2 cups all-purpose flour, sifted

2 teaspoons baking powder
1 teaspoon salt
4 egg whites
2 teaspoons grated lemon peel

Cream together margarine and sugar. Add egg yolks. Beat and add lemon juice alternately with sifted all-purpose flour, baking powder and salt. Mix well after each addition. Beat egg whites until stiff and fold in lemon peel and then fold whites into creamed mixture. Fill greased muffin cups ¾ full. Bake 20 minutes at 375°.

MAKES 12 MUFFINS.

Chef's Hint: These muffins freeze well.

Authors' Tip: Do not use diet margarine when preparing this recipe.

CANTALOUPE MOUSSE

2 envelopes unflavored gelatin
¼ cup cold water
½ medium cantaloupe, seeded, pared, and puréed

2 cups heavy cream
2 cups sugar
4 egg whites, at room temperature

Sprinkle gelatin over cold water to soften. In a double boiler stir over hot water to dissolve gelatin. Cool and add to the melon. Beat cream until soft peaks form. Gradually add one cup sugar. Beat egg whites till fluffy. Gradually add 1 cup sugar. Fold together cream and egg whites and fold into melon. Chill 1 hour.

SERVES 8 GENEROUSLY.

CRUNCHY BAKED BANANAS

2 large or 3 medium bananas
2 tablespoons brown sugar
½ cup miniature marshmallows

1 cup corn flakes
1 tablespoon melted margarine

Peel and cut bananas lengthwise. Put in a buttered dish. Sprinkle with brown sugar and top with marshmallows. Mix cornflakes and margarine. Sprinkle over bananas. Bake 12 minutes at 375°.

SERVES 4.

Authors' Tip: Delicious served over ice cream.

PINE RIDGE INN

2893 West Pine Street • Mount Airy, North Carolina 27030 • (910) 789-5034 • Manford and Ellen Haxton

In 1948, the United States was enjoying the prosperous peace that followed World War II. Under President Harry Truman, the country bustled with activity. The average American household was learning about new conveniences, like the automatic dishwasher, that made life easier, and television that brought entertainment into every living room. In this time of growth and change, a lavish mansion was constructed in the shadows of the Blue Ridge Mountains. The original owner of the mansion died and left it to his son, who converted it into an inn to make it more marketable. The present owners bought it twelve years ago. Today, it is the Pine Ridge Inn.

Visitors to the inn experience a unique combination of elegance and coziness. In its picturesque rooms, original art, fresh flowers, and potted plants complement museum-quality antiques. You can relax in the library or soothe yourself in the indoor hot tub. The inn also offers an exercise room with Nautilus equipment and an outdoor swimming pool. Golf privileges are available at the Cross Creek Country Club.

Mount Airy is known for a variety of reasons. It is the site of the world's largest open-face granite quarry. It also gained fame as the hometown of television's Andy of Mayberry and Matlock — actor Andy Griffith — and of country music singer Donna Fargo. The town's many outlet stores have made it a mecca for bargain hunters.

Pine Ridge is just 15 minutes from the Blue Ridge Parkway and Pilot Mountain, a popular local landmark that offers spectacular views from its summit. An hour's drive will take you to Winston-Salem and Greensboro; High Point and Charlotte are also within comfortable driving distance.

BREAKFAST PIZZA

1 package (9 or 10 ounces) refrigerated crescent rolls
1 cup browned sausage
1 cup crisp bacon, crumbled (divided)
1 cup hash browned potatoes

1 cup shredded Cheddar cheese (divided)
5 eggs
¼ cup milk
Salt and pepper to taste

Unroll crescent rolls and place on a greased 13x9-inch pan. On top of the rolls spread sausage, ½ cup bacon, potatoes, and ½ cup cheese. Beat eggs and add milk and pour over the above. Add the remaining bacon and cheese. Sprinkle with salt and pepper. Bake at 350° for 30 minutes or until lightly browned.
SERVES 12.

Authors' Tip: This is a terrific recipe to make for kids. It's firm enough to pick up and eat with fingers. It also could be cut into small pieces and served as hors d'oeuvre.

FABULOUS FUDGE BROWNIES

1 box brownie mix
½ cup water

½ cup applesauce
1 egg

Preheat oven to 350°. Grease bottom of 13x9-inch pan. Mix brownie mix, water, applesauce, and egg in a large bowl. Beat 50 strokes by hand. Do not undermix. Spread in greased pan. Bake for 33-35 minutes. Do not overbake. Cool completely and store covered.
SERVES 12 TO 15.

Easy Ready Muffins

1 15-ounce box Raisin Bran
cereal (add extra raisins if
desired)
3 cups sugar
5 cups all-purpose flour
5 teaspoons baking soda or
3 teaspoons baking powder and
2 tablespoons baking soda

1 tablespoon pumpkin pie spice
2 teaspoons salt
4 eggs (can use an egg substitute
substitute)
1 cup margarine, melted
2 teaspoons vanilla
1 quart buttermilk

Mix bran, sugar, flour, soda, salt, and spices. Add eggs, margarine, vanilla, and buttermilk. Mix well. Store in covered dish in refrigerator. Bake in muffin pan at 400° for about 13 minutes. Will keep six weeks.

Makes 24 muffins.

Authors' Tip: This recipe yields a very large amount of batter. Just use the amount desired and keep the rest in the refrigerator ready to bake whenever you wish.

Whole-Wheat Oven Pancakes

1 cup whole-wheat flour
1 cup bran cereal
⅓ cup wheat germ
1½ teaspoons baking powder
½ teaspoon baking soda

1 egg
1 cup buttermilk
¼ cup hot water
¼ cup oil
¼ cup honey

Mix together flour, cereal, wheat germ, baking powder, and soda. Add egg, buttermilk, water, oil, and honey. Beat well. Spread batter evenly in greased 15x10x1-inch pan. Bake in a 425° oven for 12 minutes.

Serves 8 to 10.

$\mathcal{K}$ING'S ARMS

*212 Pollock Street • New Bern, North Carolina 28560 • (919) 638-4409 or (800) 872-9306
• Richard and Patricia Gulley*

$\mathcal{T}$he King's Arms takes its name from a tavern in New Bern that is said to have hosted members of the First Continental Congress. The inn is a short carriage ride from Governor Tryon's Palace, the handsomely restored governor's residence during the pre-Revolutionary Royal Colony of Carolina. Situated near the meeting point of the Neuse and Trent Rivers, the house was constructed by John Alexander Meadows in 1847—"five bays wide, single pile with a gable roof, and interior chimneys." Enlarged considerably in 1895, it was established as a Colonial inn in 1980.

Each spacious guest room has a lovely fireplace, private bath, and is individually furnished with period antiques and reproductions. Breakfast is served to your room. You'll enjoy juice, hot beverage and, according to the baker's whim, a variety of fresh breads or biscuits.

In addition to Tryon Palace, the New Bern Historic District now includes more than 180 structures and residences listed on the National Register. Many of these architectural treasures date as early as 1780. For sporting enthusiasts, the Gulleys will be happy to arrange tee times, tennis court dates, or to direct you to nearby hunting, fishing, boating and sailing sources.

KING'S ARMS CRANBERRY MUFFINS

2 eggs
½ cup milk
½ cup oil
1 teaspoon vanilla
2 cups all-purpose flour

1 cup sugar
2½ teaspoons baking powder
1 teaspoon salt
1 cup chopped fresh cranberries
1½ cup pecans (optional)

Beat eggs in small bowl. Add wet ingredients and blend. Set aside. In separate bowl, mix dry ingredients. Form well in center of dry ingredients and add wet mixture. Stir only to blend lightly. Add chopped cranberries and nuts. Bake at 375° for 17 to 20 minutes.

MAKES 12 MUFFINS.

KOLACKYS

1 cup (2 sticks) corn oil
   margarine, at room temperature
1 8-ounce package cream cheese,
   softened
2 tablespoons sugar

2 cups all-purpose flour
2 teaspoons baking powder
1/4 teaspoon salt
   Assorted preserves or jellies
   Powdered sugar

Thoroughly blend margarine, cream cheese, and sugar. Add flour, baking powder, and salt and mix well. Knead to form a stiff dough. Roll to 1/4-inch thickness. Cut out with a biscuit cutter and place on a greased baking sheet. Indent centers and fill with preserves. Bake at 350° for 20 minutes. Sprinkle with powdered sugar.

MAKES 4 DOZEN.

Chef's Note: These are a holiday favorite at our house and at the inn.

ALLISON MARIE COOKIES

1 cup butter (at room temperature)
1 cup sugar
1 cup light brown sugar, lightly packed
1 cup vegetable oil
2 eggs
1 teaspoon vanilla extract

3½ cups all-purpose flour
1 teaspoon salt
1 teaspoon baking soda
1 teaspoon cream of tartar
1 cup Rice Krispies
1 cup quick oats
1 cup shredded coconut
1 cup chopped nuts

In a large bowl, cream together the butter, sugar, brown sugar, and oil. In another bowl beat together well the eggs and vanilla extract and add to the sugar mixture. Next mix together well the flour, salt, baking soda, and cream of tartar and add to the sugar-and-egg mixture. Stir in the Rice Krispies, oats, coconut, and chopped nuts. Place by spoonfuls on an ungreased cookie sheet. Flatten each spoonful slightly. Bake at 350° for 5 to 6 minutes. Reverse the pans and bake approximately 5 to 6 minutes more.

MAKES ABOUT 10 DOZEN COOKIES.

Chef's Note: This recipe was named for my daughter for her baptism on January 15, 1994.

NEW BERNE HOUSE

709 Broad Street • New Bern, North Carolina 28560 • (919) 636-2250 or (800) 842-7688
• Marcia Drum and Howard Bronson

A visit to this splendidly restored Colonial Revival home with its charming porch and garden is like a step into yesteryear. Seven lovely guest rooms are decorated in English country style. The home's attic finds include a "notorious" brass bed that was reportedly rescued from a burning brothel in 1897.

From New Berne House, you can easily walk to Tryon Palace and its formal gardens and other historic sites. Or take a horse-drawn carriage for a complete tour of the 40-block historic district and waterfront. History, as well as quaint shops and fine restaurants, await your pleasure.

A day at New Berne House begins with a full breakfast served in the formal dining room. The inn is known for its breakfast treats which may include luscious praline and cream waffles or spiced apple crepes with cream cheese topping. Two weekends each month, the inn is reserved for a juicy whodunit mystery package, which fits nicely with the house's two "haunted" guest rooms. Marcia and Howard tells us that "guests have reported 'odd occurrences' over the years."

PICED BACON

1 pound bacon	1 teaspoon cinnamon
1 cup light brown sugar	3 tablespoons water

Layer bacon with paper towel on microwaveable dish. Cook half the normal time. Remove and blot on a clean paper towel. Wash and dry dish and arrange the bacon in a single layer on the dish without a paper towel. Mix the remaining ingredients together until it is a thick syrup consistency. Brush the cinnamon mixture on the bacon. Return the bacon to the microwave and finish cooking. Drain on pastry rack.

SERVES 4 TO 6.

REAKFAST BREAD

4 cups bread cubes	1 teaspoon cinnamon
4 eggs	⅛ teaspoon nutmeg
2 cups half-and-half	⅛ teaspoon ground cloves
1 teaspoon vanilla extract	⅛ teaspoon ginger

Beat eggs and cream until well blended. Add extract and spices, pour over bread and let stand 20 minutes. Pour into 9x5x2-inch lightly oiled loaf pan. Bake at 350° for 40 to 45 minutes or until a knife blade inserted in the center comes out clean.

Slice and serve with syrup as French Toast or spoon into cereal bowls and serve with berries and cream as Bread Pudding.

MAKES 1 LOAF.

Chef's Hint: Egg substitute and skimmed milk turns this into a dietary delight.

GRANDVIEW LODGE

*809 Valley View Circle Road • Waynesville, North Carolina 28786 • (704) 456-5212 or
(800) 255-7826 • Stan and Linda Arnold*

*P*ick one of the comfortable rocking chairs that line the porch of the lodge, settle back and soak in the view. Located in the Great Smoky Mountains, just outside the quaint town of Waynesville, Grandview Lodge sits on two and a half rolling acres graced with apple orchards, grape arbors, and rhubarb patches.

Delicious food is the hallmark of this inn. Linda seems to mix her own special magic into every recipe. She usually plans her menus around the harvest of locally grown fruits, vegetables, and herbs. Breads, muffins, and biscuits are all home-baked, and jellies, jams, and relishes are homemade, too. The lodge's spacious dining room with its large tables is a wonderful place to share good conversation and delicious food.

By the way, Stan speaks Polish, Russian, German, and Hebrew, and Linda is a chef, author, and graduate home economist. She will be glad to satisfy special dietary requirements if you give advance notice.

It's a short drive from Grandview Lodge to Maggie Valley, the Cherokee Indian Reservation, the Biltmore House, the Blue Ridge Parkway, and the Great Smoky Mountains National Park, so you won't run short of interesting things to do and see.

ℬAKED HAM

Place a smoked ham fat side up on a rack in a shallow pan. Insert meat thermometer in the thickest part, away from the bone. Bake in a 325° oven to an internal temperature of 130°, 15 minutes per pound. Remove from oven and let stand 15 minutes before carving.

Gravy

Pour drippings from pan into a large measuring cup. Pour water into the pan, scraping crusty bits from pan. Drain and reserve water. For 2 cups of gravy, heat 3 tablespoons of fat from measuring cup, discarding remaining fat. Stir in ¼ cup flour and cook, stirring constantly, about 2 minutes. Stir in 2 cups of liquid (drippings plus water from deglazing pan). Season with salt and pepper to taste. Simmer and stir 2 to 3 minutes.

Chef's Hint: Freeze unused water from pan. Can be used to cook rice or a pot of soup.

Au Jus

Pour drippings from pan into a large measuring cup. Skim fat and discard. Pour water into pan, scraping crusty bits from the bottom. For 2 cups of au jus, combine 1 cup of drippings with 1 cup of water from deglazing pan. Heat and season with salt and pepper to taste.

AGUETTES

½ cup warm water (105° to 115°F.)
1 tablespoon (¼ -ounce packet) active dry yeast
2 teaspoons sugar

2 teaspoons shortening or oil
3 to 4 cups bread flour
1½ teaspoons salt
1 cup water

In a measuring cup dissolve yeast and sugar in ½ cup warm water. Set aside to proof while assembling other ingredients. If using a dough hook, combine 3 cups of flour, salt, and shortening in mixing bowl. Add proofed yeast and an additional cup of water slowly while mixer is running. Add more all-purpose flour to make a stiff dough. Knead for 10 minutes.

If kneading by hand, beat together proofed yeast, shortening, salt, water, and 1 cup of all-purpose flour. Gradually add flour to make a stiff dough. Knead 10 to 15 minutes on a lightly floured surface incorporating as little extra flour as possible.

Place dough in a bowl and cover with plastic wrap; let rise 1½ hours. Punch down and knead back into a ball, cover, and let rise again. Second rising will probably take only 1 hour. Punch down and divide dough in half. Shape each half into a long sausage shape. Place in a greased baguette pan or on a greased baking sheet. Let rise in warm place 1 hour. Bake in preheated 400° oven with a pan of water for 15 minutes. Remove pan of water and continue baking 20-30 minutes until golden brown. Remove bread and cool on wire rack.

MAKES 2 BAGUETTES.

LINDA'S BREAD

1 tablespoon (¼-ounce packet) active dry yeast	¾ cup bran cereal
1 cup warm water (105°-115°)	¾ cup rolled oats
1 tablespoon sugar	¾ cup bread flour
⅓ cup dry milk powder	3 tablespoons brown sugar
¾ cup whole-wheat flour	1 teaspoon salt
	3 tablespoons shortening or oil

In a 2-cup measure or small bowl dissolve yeast and 1 tablespoon sugar in warm water. Set aside to proof while assembling other ingredients.

If using a dough hook, combine all dry ingredients and shortening in mixing bowl. Add proofed yeast slowly while mixer is running. Add more bread flour by tablespoons if dough is too sticky or more water by tablespoon if dough is too crumbly. Knead for 10 minutes. This mixed grain dough will be softer and stickier than all white.

If kneading by hand, beat together proofed yeast, shortening, salt, brown sugar, and dry milk. Stir in mixed grains, adding bread flour last. Knead by hand 10-15 minutes on a slightly floured surface, incorporating as little extra flour as possible.

Place dough in bowl and cover with towel or plastic wrap; set in warm area away from draft. Let rise 1½ hours. Punch down and knead briefly; cover and let rise again. Second rising will probably take only 1 hour. Punch down and place dough on clean surface. Flatten dough into a 6x12-inch rectangle. Starting at 6 inch side, roll dough in jellyroll fashion stretching dough slightly. This will help eliminate big holes in bread. Tuck ends under and place dough in a greased loaf pan seam side down. Cover lightly with plastic wrap and let rise in warm place one hour.

Bake in preheated 425° oven for 10 minutes; reduce temperature to 375° and bake 30 minutes or until bread is browned and sounds hollow when tapped. Remove bread from pan and cool on wire rack. Wrap in foil. Slice bread and store in freezer.

MAKES 1 LOAF.

Chef's Note: This is a dense bread high in protein and fiber.

$\mathscr{C}$INNAMON BUNS

1 tablespoon (¼-ounce packet)
  active dry yeast
1 tablespoon sugar
¼ cup warm water (105° to 115°F)
3¼ cups all-purpose flour
4 tablespoons butter or
  margarine, softened

2 tablespoons shortening
1 teaspoon salt
2 eggs
⅓ cup milk

Stir the yeast and sugar into the warm water; let stand 5 minutes. If using a food processor, process flour, margarine, shortening, and salt for 20 seconds. With the machine running, add eggs, milk, and yeast mixture in a steady stream. Process for 40 seconds.

Scrape dough into a 3-quart mixing bowl. Cover with plastic wrap and refrigerate 4-6 hours. Punch down and use immediately or return to refrigerator for up to 4 days. Punch down again just before using.

Filling
3 tablespoons butter or
  margarine, softened
⅓ cup firmly packed brown sugar
1 teaspoon cinnamon

Glaze
½ cup firmly packed brown sugar
½ cup butter or margarine
  (1 stick)
3 tablespoons maple flavored
  syrup
⅓ cup chopped pecans
1 tablespoon grated orange peel
  (optional)

Turn dough out onto a floured surface. Roll into a 16x12 inch rectangle and spread with softened butter. Combine brown sugar and cinnamon; sprinkle over dough. Starting at long edge, roll up dough, jellyroll fashion; press seam to seal. Cut into 16 slices.

Grease a 12x7x2 pan. Combine brown sugar, margarine, and syrup for glaze; beat until fluffy. Add nuts and orange peel. Spread glaze evenly over bottom of pan. Place slices of dough over glaze. Cover and place in refrigerator overnight. Remove from refrigerator in morning and place in warm place to rise two hours. Bake in preheated 375° oven for 30-35 minutes. Cool two minutes. Invert pan onto platter; do not remove pan for 1-2 minutes so that glaze can run down sides.

MAKES 16 BUNS.

HONEY-WHEAT ROLLS

1 tablespoon (¼-ounce packet)
  active dry yeast
½ cup warm water (105° to 115°)
1 teaspoon sugar
2 cups whole-wheat flour
1 teaspoon salt

½ cup butter or margarine
  (1 stick), softened
12 ounces cottage cheese
3 tablespoons honey
1 egg

In a measuring cup dissolve yeast in warm water with sugar. Set aside while assembling other ingredients. If you have a mixer with a dough hook, put all remaining ingredients in mixing bowl. Add proofed yeast and knead with dough hook for about 10 minutes adding more bread flour or water to make a soft, elastic dough.

If kneading by hand, put all wet ingredients in large mixing bowl. Beating with a wooden spoon, add flour ½ cup at a time. Knead by hand 10-15 minutes on a lightly floured surface.

Cover bowl with towel or plastic wrap; set in warm area away from draft. Let rise 1½ hours. Punch down and shape into rolls on a greased baking sheet. Set pan in warm area free of draft. Let rise about 1 hour. Bake in preheated 375° oven for 15-18 minutes until lightly browned.

MAKES ABOUT 24 ROLLS.

EAST ROLLS

1 tablespoon (¼-ounce packet) active dry yeast	¼ cup shortening
½ cup warm water (105° to 115°)	1 teaspoon salt
3 tablespoons sugar	½ cup milk
1 egg	3 to 3½ cups bread flour

Dissolve yeast and 1 tablespoon sugar in warm water. Set aside to proof while assembling other ingredients.

In a large mixing bowl combine remaining ingredients with one cup of flour. Mix well. Add proofed yeast and enough flour to make a soft dough. Knead by hand for 15 minutes or knead 10 minutes if using a dough hook. Place kneaded dough in a large bowl and cover with plastic wrap. Place bowl in a warm place away from drafts.

Let dough rise 1½ hours until doubled in bulk. Punch down and shape into rolls. Place on a greased baking sheet and let rise 1 hour. Bake in a pre-heated 375° oven for 15 to 18 minutes until browned.

MAKES ABOUT 24 ROLLS.

*B*ANANA NUT BREAD

3 large, very ripe bananas	2 cups all-purpose flour
½ cup oil	1 teaspoon baking soda
2 eggs	½ teaspoon baking powder
1 cup sugar	3 tablespoons buttermilk
1 teaspoon vanilla	½ cup chopped pecans

In large mixing bowl combine bananas, oil, eggs, sugar, vanilla. Beat well about 3 minutes. Add remaining ingredients, mixing well.

Pour into greased 9x5x3-inch loaf pan. Bake in preheated 325° for 50 to 60 minutes until lightly browned and bread pulls away slightly from pan. Cool on rack. Wrap in foil and serve next day.

MAKES ONE LOAF.

Variation: Use half whole-wheat flour and reduce sugar to ½ cup.

Chef's Hint: Don't have 3 ripe bananas today? Place bananas in freezer, skin and all. Thaw in a bowl, discarding skin when thawed.

CORNBREAD

1 cup yellow cornmeal	½ teaspoon baking soda
1 cup all-purpose flour	1 cup buttermilk
2 tablespoons sugar	⅓ cup butter or margarine, melted
4 teaspoons baking powder	1 egg

Combine all dry ingredients in a mixing bowl. Stir in remaining ingredients. Beat vigorously about ½ minute. Pour into greased square pan. Bake in preheated 425° oven for 20 to 25 minutes until browned.

Serves 9.

Chef's Hint: Oil can be substituted for the butter but the bread will not be as golden.

CORN STICKS

1 cup cornmeal	1 cup buttermilk
3 tablespoons all-purpose flour	1 egg
1 teaspoon baking powder	3 tablespoons butter or
¼ teaspoon baking soda	margarine, melted

Preheat oven to 450°. Grease a cornstick pan generously with solid butter or margarine. Place greased pan in oven. Meanwhile, in a mixing bowl combine all dry ingredients. Stir in remaining ingredients. Beat vigorously about ½ minute. Spoon batter into hot prepared pans. Return pans to 450° oven for 12 to 15 minutes until golden brown.

MAKES ABOUT 12 STICKS.

Chef's Hint: Do not substitute an aerosol vegetable spray for the butter or margarine. You can use a vegetable oil for greasing the pan.

RAN MUFFINS

1½ cups bran cereal (100% Bran)
1 cup milk
1 cup all-purpose flour
⅓ cup sugar

2½ teaspoons baking powder
½ teaspoon baking soda
1 egg
¼ cup oil

In a medium bowl combine bran with milk. Let stand 5 minutes while combining dry ingredients. Stir egg and oil into bran mixture. Stir in flour mixture just until moistened; do not beat. Fill 12 well-greased muffin cups ⅔ full. Bake in preheated 400° oven for 20 minutes or until tester comes clean.
MAKES 12 MUFFINS.

UMPKIN/SWEET POTATO MUFFINS

¾ cup brown sugar
½ cup butter (1 stick), softened
¼ cup molasses
1 egg
1 cup pumpkin or sweet potato
  purée

1¾ cup all-purpose flour
1 teaspoon baking soda
½ cup chopped pecans or raisins

In a mixing bowl combine first 5 ingredients, beating until smooth. Stir in flour and remaining ingredients. Spoon into greased muffin pans. Bake in preheated 400° oven for 15 to 18 minutes.
MAKES 12 TO 15 MUFFINS.

APPLE OATMEAL MUFFINS

1 cup plus 2 tablespoons rolled oats
1 cup buttermilk
1 teaspoon vanilla
1 egg
¾ cup light brown sugar
⅓ cup butter or margarine, melted
½ cup all-purpose flour
½ cup whole-wheat flour

2½ teaspoons baking powder
½ teaspoon baking soda
1 teaspoon salt (optional)
½ teaspoon cinnamon
½ teaspoon nutmeg
¼ cup chopped pecans
6- ounce (1 large) tart apple, unpeeled, chopped

In mixing bowl combine oatmeal, buttermilk, and vanilla. Let stand five minutes. Add egg, brown sugar, and melted butter. Mix well. Add remaining ingredients. Mix lightly until all ingredients are moistened. Spoon batter into greased muffin pans. Bake in preheated 400° oven for 15 to 18 minutes until lightly browned.

MAKES 12 VERY LARGE MUFFINS OR 18 REGULAR MUFFINS.

Variation: Use 2 large ripe bananas instead of apple.

BUTTERMILK BISCUITS

2¼ cups self-rising flour
1 teaspoon sugar
¼ teaspoon baking soda

⅓ cup shortening
¾ cup buttermilk

In a large bowl combine flour, sugar, and soda. Stir with a fork. Cut in shortening with 2 knives or pastry blender until the consistency of coarse meal. Add buttermilk, stirring no more than 25 times and dough forms a soft, moist ball. Knead slightly on a floured surface. Roll out to ½ inch thickness. Fold dough in half and roll out again to ½ inch thickness. Cut with floured biscuit cutter or a glass. Place on an ungreased baking sheet. If each biscuit touches, the sides will be soft; if not touching, the sides will be crispy.

Bake in preheated 450° oven for 12 to 15 minutes until light brown. Serve immediately.

MAKES ABOUT 20 2-INCH BISCUITS.

CRANBERRY SALAD

1 can (8¾-ounce) crushed pineapple
1 package (3-ounce) raspberry gelatin
  orange juice

1 cup fresh or frozen cranberries
1 rib celery
1 whole orange, unpeeled, seeded
½ cup chopped pecans

Drain pineapple, reserving liquid. Add enough orange juice to make 1 cup liquid. Bring liquid to a boil and stir into gelatin until gelatin dissolves. Chill until slightly thickened. The chilling process can be shortened by setting the bowl in ice water.

Meanwhile, using a food processor or food grinder chop cranberries, celery, and orange. Add all ingredients to gelatin. Stir gelatin and chopped fruit together. Pour into a 4-cup mold or 6 to 8 individual molds.

SERVES 8.

Chef's Hint: Keep cranberries in the freezer all year round so this recipe is not limited to Thanksgiving and Christmas.

Authors' Tip: If desired, a jar of cranberry-orange relish can be substituted for the fresh cranberries and whole orange.

FROZEN CRANBERRY SALAD

2 3-ounce packages cream cheese, softened
2 tablespoons sugar
2 tablespoons mayonnaise
1 can (16-ounce) whole cranberry sauce
1 can (8¾ ounce) crushed pineapple, drained

½ cup chopped nuts
1 cup whipping cream, whipped, or 2 cups whipped cream or topping
4 drops red food coloring

In a mixing bowl, cream together cream cheese, sugar and mayonnaise. Stir in cranberry sauce, pineapple, and nuts. Fold in whipped cream and food coloring. Pour into loaf pan or individual molds. Freeze until firm. Let stand 10 to 15 minutes at room temperature. Unmold.

MAKES 8 TO 10 SERVINGS.

FRUIT SALAD

3 cups fruit for salad or fruit
  cocktail, drained
½ cup shredded coconut
½ cup miniature marshmallows

1 cup sour cream or vanilla
  yogurt
¼ teaspoon cinnamon

Combine all ingredients. Cover and chill several hours or overnight.
SERVES 6.
Authors' Tip: Top with fruit yogurt dressing or whipped cream and garnish with a sprig of mint and/or red cherries.

FRUIT YOGURT DRESSING

⅓ cup sugar
2 tablespoons orange peel
¾ cup plain yogurt
¼ cup oil
2 tablespoons fruit flavored
  vinegar or cider vinegar

2 tablespoons orange juice
  concentrate
1 tablespoon poppy seeds
  (optional)
¼ teaspoon salt

Combine all ingredients in jar with tight-fitting lid and shake well. Store in refrigerator.
MAKES ABOUT 1½ CUPS.

Chef's Note: This dressing goes well with a winter citrus combination or a summer berry and melon combination.

ALDORF SALAD

Salad
- 1 rib celery, chopped
- ½ cup raisins
- ½ cup toasted broken pecans
- 1 tart red apple, chopped
- 1 small banana, sliced (optional)

Combine all ingredients with dressing. Chill.
SERVES 4 TO 6.

Chef's Note: This cooked dressing is much lower in fat than mayonnaise and cream combination.

Dressing
- 1 egg
- ⅓ to ½ cup sugar
- 2 tablespoons lemon juice

In small saucepan beat ingredients together. Cook until thickened over medium heat stirring constantly. Cool.

MINIATURE CHEESECAKES

Cakes
- 1 pound cream cheese, softened
- ¾ cup sugar
- 2 eggs
- 1 tablespoon lemon juice
- 1 teaspoon vanilla extract
  Vanilla wafers

Topping
- 1 cup sour cream
- 2 tablespoons sugar
- ½ teaspoon vanilla extract
- 1 can (16-ounce) cherry pie filling

In a mixing bowl, combine first 5 ingredients and beat at medium speed until well mixed. Use the gem-size muffin pan for truly bite size. Use paper liners and place one wafer in each liner. Spoon cheese mixture over wafers. Bake in preheated 350° oven for 15 minutes. Meanwhile, combine sour cream, sugar, and vanilla. Spoon onto baked cheesecakes. Return to oven for 5 minutes. Cool to room temperature. Spoon pie filling over cheesecakes. Chill.
MAKES ABOUT 24 CHEESECAKES.

Chef's Hint: For variations try blueberry pie filling, strawberry preserves, fresh strawberries, and shaved chocolate.

THE SWAG COUNTRY INN

*Hemphill Road • Route 2, Box 280-A • Waynesville, North Carolina 28786 • (704) 926-0430 or
(704) 926-3119 • Deener Matthews*

The Swag is located at the top of a 5,000-foot private mountain at the edge of the Great Smoky Mountain National Park. A charming country inn on 250 acres of pristine meadows and woods, the Swag's buildings were constructed of hand-hewn logs retrieved from Appalachian structures, including a century-old church that forms the core of the main building. From its massive stone fireplace in the living room to its North Carolina arts and crafts, the inn is an enchanting blend of mountain authenticity and rustic elegance.

Guest rooms and cabins are individually decorated with handmade quilts, woven rugs, and works of art. Most rooms feature private balconies and fireplaces. The Swag has a private entrance to the national park with its many long and short trails for hiking. You may come upon cascading waterfalls on your walk, and perhaps plan a picnic on a mountain top.

Dining is sensational at the Swag, where regional cuisine is presented with imaginative and innovative flair. Breakfast begins with a selection of homemade granola, hot apple-spiced oatmeal, muffins and cinnamon bread. Freshly squeezed orange juice, seasonal fruits, French toast, blueberry pancakes, or a special egg dish complete this most delicious start to the day.

MARY POPE'S CHOCOLATE MOUSSE

8 ounces best quality semisweet
  chocolate

8 eggs
¼ cup rum

Melt the chocolate in a double boiler. Separate yolks and whites. Add rum to yolks. Whisk yolks and rum together over boiling water in a metal bowl until mixture is frothy. (Be careful to whisk constantly or you'll get scrambled eggs). Fold in warm melted chocolate. Beat egg whites until stiff. Fold whites into chocolate egg mixture. Chill for at least two hours.
SERVES 6 TO 8.

MRS. MAC'S BRANDY SNAPS

½ cup molasses
½ cup butter (1 stick)
¾ cup all-purpose flour

⅔ cup sugar
Pinch salt
1 to 2 teaspoons powdered ginger

Heat molasses to boiling point. Melt the butter in the molasses. Slowly add pre-sifted dry ingredients and stir until well combined. Grease the backside of a cookie sheet. Drop from a small teaspoon at least 2 inches apart onto cookie sheet. The mixture will spread out a lot. Cool slightly until it can be removed with a metal spatula.
SERVES 6 TO 8.

SWAG CHOCOLATE MOUSSE NAPOLEON

Assemble the Napoleon by combining the Chocolate Mousse (recipe above) layered with the Brandy Snaps (recipe above).

To serve dessert, paint chocolate sauce on a plate. Place the mousse in a pastry bag and pipe out onto plate in a small round circle. Add brandy snap, more mousse, another brandy snap, whipped cream, and a sprig of fresh mint. If you feel brave, try three or perhaps even four tiers!

SERVES 8 TO 10.

Chef's Note: Chef Rolf Nelson grew up in England and New York City. "Two people who influenced my life and my cooking were my English grandmother, Mary Pope and our next-door neighbor Mrs. MacMullen. Both have since passed away but left me with a few recipes that are superb. To create the Swag Chocolate Mousse Napoleon, I delved into my past and combined two of my favorite desserts from two of my favorite people."

𝒯HE RHETT HOUSE INN

1009 Craven Street • Beaufort, South Carolina 29002 • (803) 524-9030 • Steve and Marianne Harrison

𝒜 stay at this inn will take you back to gracious antebellum days, when aristocrat Thomas Rhett and his wife, Caroline Barnwell, lived in the house before the Civil War. The Rhett House, like many of Beaufort's historic sites, was saved by Union troops who occupied the town.

The Harrisons go out of their way to assure the comfort of their guests. You will find freshly cut flowers, as well as all modern amenities, in the elegantly furnished guest rooms. Their living room is filled with American and English antiques. The inn is just a block from Beaufort's bustling waterfront where you can enjoy a stroll and watch the traffic on the intercoastal waterway. After a day of sightseeing, you might enjoy a glass of wine while you relax on the wraparound porch. Afternoon tea, with treats including linzer tortes or homemade chocolate chip cookies, is served by the fire or on the verandah. Your rates include accommodations, afternoon tea, a full breakfast, and bicycles for your explorations of the town.

Beaufort is the birthplace of novelist Pat Conroy, who set *The Great Santini* in his home town. When Conroy's *Prince of Tides* was filmed here, Barbra Streisand and Nick Nolte stayed at The Rhett House Inn. The lovely town was also the setting for *The Big Chill*. As you sightsee among its beautiful antebellum mansions, under magnificent oaks and Spanish moss canopies, you will understand why Beaufort is a favorite locale for Hollywood filmmakers.

*S*HRIMP AND SCALLOP CEVICHE

3 pounds shrimp	1 avocado, diced fine
3 pounds scallops	½ bunch Italian parsley (minced)
1 pint lime juice	3 large sweet potatoes, cooked
1 cup Sauterne wine	1 dozen Belgian endive leaves
½ medium jalapeño pepper	1 lemon peel, cut julienne
1 red pepper, diced fine	1 lime peel, cut julienne
½ red onion, diced fine	

Blanch shrimp and scallops. Cool immediately; drain and chill. Combine lime juice, Sauterne, and jalapeño pepper and add to scallops and shrimp. Combine red pepper, onion, avocado, and parsley together. Scoop the three large sweet potatoes with a baller. Line the plate with endive spears. Place three ounces of scallop mixture on endive spears. Add avocado mixture and sweet potatoes. Sprinkle with lemon peel and lime peel.
SERVES 8 TO 10.

*S*TRAWBERRY YOGURT MUFFINS

1½ cups unbleached flour	½ cup sugar
¼ teaspoon salt	½ teaspoon vanilla extract
½ teaspoon cream of tartar	2 eggs
¼ teaspoon baking soda	¼ cup plain yogurt
½ cup unsalted butter	⅔ cup chopped fresh strawberries

Preheat oven to 400°. Grease muffin cups. To prepare muffins, in a bowl, sift together the flour, salt, cream of tartar, and soda. Cream the butter and sugar in a large bowl until fluffy. Add the vanilla, then add the eggs one at a time, beating well after each addition. Alternately add dry ingredients and yogurt to creamed mixture. Gently fold in strawberries. Spoon into a muffin tin to ⅔ full and bake for 25 minutes or until golden brown. Allow muffins to cool on a rack for 10 minutes before removing from pan.

Makes 12 muffins.

Chef's Note: For Blueberry Muffins use 1 cup whole blueberries instead of strawberries or to make Raspberry Muffins use ⅔ cup whole raspberries.

PEAR MUFFINS

2 cups unbleached flour, sifted	½ cup sugar
1 teaspoon baking powder	2 eggs
½ teaspoon baking soda	½ cup plain yogurt
¼ teaspoon salt	½ cup milk
¼ teaspoon cinnamon	1 cup peeled and chopped ripe
¼ teaspoon allspice	pears
½ cup salted butter, softened	½ teaspoon almond extract

Preheat the oven to 400°. Grease the muffin pan. Prepare the muffins. Sift together the flour, baking powder, soda, salt, cinnamon, and allspice. In a large bowl, cream the butter. Add the sugar and beat until fluffy. Add eggs, one at a time, beating after each addition. Add the dry ingredients to the creamed mixture alternately with the yogurt and milk. Gently stir in pears and almond extract. Spoon into pan to ⅔ full and bake for 20 to 25 minutes or until a wooden toothpick inserted in center comes clean. Cool on a wire rack for 5 minutes before removing from pans. Serve warm.

Makes 12 muffins.

1837 BED & BREAKFAST

126 Wentworth Street • Charleston, South Carolina 29401 • (803) 723-7166 • Sherri Weaver and Richard Dunn

$\mathscr{B}$uilt circa 1800, this former cotton planter's home with its brick carriage house offers inviting guest rooms furnished and decorated with carefully chosen antiques, period pieces, and works of art. Rockers on the open verandahs provide a charming place to relax and savor the Southern hospitality.

Each day at the inn begins with a hearty gourmet breakfast served in the formal dining room. As you visit with other guests, you will enjoy such specialties of the house as sausage pie, eggs Benedict, ham omelets, and home-baked breads.

The 1837 B&B is situated right in Charleston's famous Historic District, so it's an easy walk to the old market, antique shops, and restaurants. You might want to take a boat tour of the city. Or arrange tours to the area's nearby beaches and plantations. Tours depart from the inn daily.

EXICAN FRITTATA

4 tablespoons margarine
½ cup onion, chopped
1 5-ounce can of corn, drained
2 4-ounce cans of green chilies, mild, drained
20 eggs
1 cup sour cream
1¼ teaspoons chili powder
½ teaspoon salt
⅓ cup all-purpose flour
12 ounces Cheddar cheese, shredded
10 ounces shredded Monterey Jack cheese
Dash red pepper
Salsa
Sour cream
Paprika

Sauté onion, corn, and chilies in margarine. Whisk eggs and sour cream together; add remaining ingredients (except salsa, sour cream, and garnish) mixing well. Combine with corn and chili mixture. Pour into two greased 10-inch glass pie plates. Bake at 325° for 40 minutes until blonde in color. Center may be runny. Cool to room temperature, cover and refrigerate.

To serve next day: Microwave each pie for one minute. Cut each frittata before baking. Bake at 325° for 40 to 45 minutes. Garnish with salsa and sour cream. Sprinkle with paprika.

Same day serving: Preheat oven to 325°. Bake for 55 minutes; center should be set and color golden brown. Slice and garnish as above.

SERVES 16.

Authors' Tip: This recipe can be halved easily.

OLLANDAISE EGGS

Sauce
- 1 package Hollandaise sauce mix
- ½ cup half-and-half
- ½ cup milk
- 8 tablespoons butter
- 2 tablespoons lemon juice

Eggs
- 16 slices of cream bread or French bread
- 19 eggs
- 4 shakes of pepper
- ¼ cup half-and-half
- 3 tablespoons margarine
- 16 ham slices
- 5 ounces Cheddar cheese, shredded

Parsley for garnish

Prepare the sauce. Follow directions on Hollandaise package until sauce thickens. Remove from heat and stir in lemon juice.

Bread may be toasted if desired.

Combine eggs, pepper, and half-and-half mixture. Mix with electric mixer until well blended. Melt margarine in frying pan. Add egg mixture. Cook on medium heat. Stir with wooden spoon until eggs are very soft but firm; moist but not runny. Should not be brown on bottom.

Place ham slice on bread covering complete surface. Generously spread Hollandaise sauce over ham. Save enough sauce to top each with approximately 1 tablespoon of sauce.

Scoop eggs generously onto bread. Do *not* mash down. Sprinkle top of eggs with cheese. Spoon on remaining Hollandaise sauce. Top with small sprig of fresh parsley. Cover with plastic wrap and refrigerate. To serve: Bake at 325° for 20 to 25 minutes, uncovered, on a greased cookie sheet.

Serves 16.

SAUSAGE PIE

Crust
- 4 eggs, beaten
- ½ cup milk
- 2 cups Bisquick
- ½ cup onion, chopped
- 2 tablespoons sesame seeds (optional)

Filling
- 2 pounds sausage, cooked
- 12 ounces sharp Cheddar cheese, shredded
- 12 ounces cottage cheese
- 8 ounces cream cheese, softened
- 4 eggs
- Sour cream for garnish
- Paprika

Prepare the crust. Combine eggs and milk; mix together. Add Bisquick and onion. Stir only until moistened. Set aside.

Prepare the filling. Brown sausage, draining well. Combine remaining ingredients, mixing well. Add sausage and eggs and mix well.

Use two glass 10-inch pie plates sprayed with cookinig oil spray. Pour ¼ of crust batter into each pie plate. Spread thinly. Add ½ of filling mixture to each pie plate. Top with remaining crust mixture. Sprinkle with sesame seeds. Bake at 350° for 40 to 45 minutes until top is golden brown. Garnish with a dollop of sour cream and a sprinkle of paprika.

SERVES 16.

Chef's Hint: This recipe may be prepared the day before serving. Cook for 30 to 35 minutes. Cool to room temperature. Cover and refrigerate. To reheat: Put into cold oven. Bake at 350° for approximately 30 minutes until golden brown.

Chef's Note: This recipe is ideal for freezing. It can be frozen in slices or whole. Decrease cooking time to 30 minutes. Cool to room temperature and package well. Will keep for up to three months.

Authors' Tip: This recipe can easily be halved. For a nice touch, garnish the pie with tomato slices and a sprig of parsley or basil.

OVERNIGHT FRENCH TOAST

Toast

12 eggs
3 cups milk
2 cups half and half
1 tablespoon vanilla
1 teaspoon cinnamon

½ teaspoon nutmeg
1 tablespoon sugar (optional)
2 French baguettes cut into
   1-inch slices or use cream bread
   (approximately 24 slices).

Mix all ingredients except bread. Spray two 10x15-inch glass casserole dishes with cooking oil spray. Place the bread in casserole dishes. Pour batter over bread; cover and refrigerate overnight. May have some batter still showing in morning—that's okay!

Topping

1 cup butter (2 sticks)
½ cup brown sugar

1 cup walnuts or pecans, finely
   ground
2 tablespoons maple syrup

Let all ingredients sit out overnight. Must be at room temperature. Spread topping over bread. Bake at 350° for 40 minutes. Serve with syrup or fruit.
Serves 12.

Chef's Note: This recipe is courtesy of Mrs. Grace Defilippo of Bethlehem, Pennsylvania.

CINNAMON SWIRL BREAD

6 tablespoons butter
⅔ cup brown sugar
⅓ cup nuts, finely chopped
5 tablespoons cinnamon

½ cup sugar
2 packages refrigerator biscuits
⅓ cup honey

Spray a bundt pan with cooking oil spray. Heat oven to 350°s.

In a saucepan over medium heat, melt butter and brown sugar until caramelized. Sprinkle some of the nuts in bundt pan and drizzle some of the brown sugar/butter mixture over the nuts. Mix cinnamon and sugar together in a plastic bag.

Cut each biscuit into 4 sections. Shake in cinnamon/sugar mixture and throw into bundt pan. After one package of biscuits is used throw in some cinnamon/sugar; drizzle with some of the brown sugar/butter mixture. Repeat with second package of biscuits.

Pour half the honey after second package of biscuits. Alternate sprinkling in nuts, cinnamon/sugar, brown sugar/butter and honey. Drizzle brown sugar/butter around edges. Bake at 350° for 30-35 minutes. Turn out of pan immediately! Bread will stick to pan if cooled in pan.

MAKES 1 LOAF.

Authors Tip: This bread is best served right out of the oven.

EMON BREAD

Bread
- 3 cups all-purpose flour
- 2 cups sugar
- 2 teaspoons baking powder
- 1 teaspoon salt
- 4 eggs
- 1 cup milk
- 1 cup vegetable oil
- 1 tablespoon grated lemon peel

Mix dry ingredients. Mix wet ingredients. Fold dry ingredients into wet. Blend until smooth.

Spray a bundt pan with cooking oil spray. Pour batter into bundt pan. Bake at 350° for 35 to 40 minutes. This bread will *not* be golden brown all over.

Glaze
- 1¼ cup sugar
- ½ cup lemon juice (from above lemons and reconstituted)

Dissolve sugar in juice over medium heat. To glaze bread, remove bread from bundt pan. Pour one half of glaze into bottom of bundt pan. Place bread back into pan. Using a butter knife, poke holes into lemon bread and pour remaining glaze over bread. Let sit briefly to absorb liquid. Sprinkle with chopped almonds.

MAKES 1 LOAF.

Chef's Hint: This bread can be frozen.

Authors' Tip: Dress up the bread for brunch or dessert by topping glaze with strawberries and filling center with whipped cream.

$\mathscr{B}$ANANA BREAD

2½ cups all-purpose flour
2 cups sugar
1½ teaspoons baking soda
1 teaspoon salt

4 eggs
1½ cups bananas, very ripe and
   mashed in food processor
1 cup margarine, melted

    Sift flour and combine all dry ingredients. Make sure there are no lumps. Combine wet ingredients; fold dry ingredients into wet. Mix well with hand mixer. Pour batter into greased bundt pan. Bake at 325° for 55 minutes. Cool to room temperature and glaze with orange-cream cheese icing.
    MAKES 2 LOAVES.

$\mathscr{O}$RANGE CREAM CHEESE ICING

8 ounces cream cheese, softened
1 box (1 pound) powdered sugar
2½ teaspoons orange extract

2 teaspoons orange peel
Half-and-half

    Beat cream cheese. Add ⅓ cup sugar and mix well. Add extract and peel. Beat. Add a little half-and-half. Then add sugar alternating until all sugar is used. Sugar should be the last ingredient added. Mixture should be thick but spreadable.
    MAKES 1½ CUPS.

PPLE YOGURT BREAD

2¼ cups all-purpose flour
2 cups sugar
½ teaspoon salt
½ teaspoon baking soda
1 teaspoon vanilla

1 cup margarine
8 ounces yogurt, plain
3 eggs
14 ounces (3 medium) apples, sliced thinly in food processor

Combine all dry ingredients. Combine all wet ingredients, except apples. Fold dry into wet ingredients. Mix well. Stir in apples and mix. Pour into greased bundt pan. *Do not allow batter to sit!* Bake at 350° for 1 hour and 10 minutes.

MAKES 1 LOAF.

Glaze
1 cup powdered sugar
1 teaspoon cinnamon

4 teaspoons milk
¼ cup nuts, finely chopped (walnuts or pecans)

Combine first 3 ingredients and pour over bread. Sprinkle with nuts.

Variation: To make vanilla glaze, substitute 1 teaspoon vanilla extract for cinnamon.

Authors' Tip: This is a beautiful sweet and moist bread that would be wonderful served at brunch.

GOLD ROOM SCONES

3½ cups all-purpose flour, unsifted
1½ teaspoons baking powder
½ cup sugar
1 teaspoon salt
½ cup margarine, at room temperature
2 eggs
1 cup milk

Combine first four ingredients. Mix by hand. *Do not use an electric mixer!* Cut the margarine into the flour mixture until texture is like cornmeal. Add eggs and milk. Stir quickly with fork until dough leaves side of bowl and forms ball. Spoon into muffin tins sprayed with cooking oil spray. Fill tins level. Bake at 350° for 15 to 20 minutes or until light brown. Remove and cool on wire racks.

MAKES 12 SCONES.

Chef's Hint: The scones can be frozen in metal tins. To reheat frozen scones, cover with paper towel and microwave on high for 50 seconds each.

LEMON CURD

3 tablespoons butter
3 eggs, beaten
1 cup sugar
4 teaspoons lemon peel
½ cup lemon juice (use fresh lemons but can supplement with reconstituted juice)

It is important to have all ingredients measured and assembled before cooking. Grate lemon peel and set aside. Fill bottom of double boiler with water and heat. Melt butter in top of double boiler over medium heat. Whisk eggs in separate bowl and add to butter, whisking continuously. Add sugar; keep whisking. Add lemon juice and peel; whisk. Keep whisking until mixture thickens, approximately 15 to 20 minutes. Pour into bowl and cool to room temperature. Refrigerate. Will keep for approximately 1 week.

MAKES 2 CUPS.

JOHN RUTLEDGE HOUSE INN

116 Broad Street • Charleston, South Carolina 29401 • (803) 723-7900 or (800) 476-9741
• Linda Bishop

$\mathcal{B}$orn into one of South Carolina's "first families," John Rutledge (1739-1800) was a gifted politician in our nation's turbulent colonial and Revolutionary times. His younger brother, Edward, was a signer of the Declaration of Independence. Elected as a delegate to the Constitutional Convention in 1787, John Rutledge traveled to Philadelphia and voted for the nation's new Constitution. President Washington appointed him Chief Justice of the Supreme Court in 1795, but his career in public service ended when the Senate failed to confirm his appointment. Ask Linda to tell you how he earned the nickname "Dictator John" while serving as President of the Republic of South Carolina.

Rutledge built this house in 1783 as a wedding gift for his bride, Elizabeth Grimke. It is one of only 15 homes belonging to signers of the Constitution that remain today, and the only one that is open to lodging guests. A rough draft of the Constitution was written in the library, which is now a sitting room for one of the inn's grand suites. The house, a national historic landmark, is handsomely furnished with period reproductions, and there is one authentic antique in each room. Nineteen guest rooms are located in the main house and two carriage houses. Guests enjoy Southern hospitality at its most elegant when wine and sherry is served in the ballroom. When you retire, you will find your bed turned down and cordial and chocolate provided. Breakfast and newspaper are delivered to your room in the morning.

The inn sits in the middle of Charleston's Historic District so that all the delights of this charming city—carriage tours, historic homes and churches, museums, galleries, and splendid shopping and restaurants—are within easy walking distance.

JOHN RUTLEDGE HOUSE INN'S SHRIMP AND GRITS

2 tablespoons butter
1 teaspoon salt
4 cups water (more if needed)

1 cup grits
½ cup cream

Add butter and salt to boiling water. Reduce heat to medium and add grits, stirring constantly. Simmer 45 minutes or more (may need to add more water). Add cream and heat gently.

¼ pound medium-size-shrimp, peeled
1 teaspoon seasoning salt
¼ cup sliced celery

Minced garlic (optional)
Grated sharp Cheddar cheese (optional)

Cook shrimp in seasoned water until pink. Sauté sliced celery in 1 tablespoon butter. If desired, may also add minced garlic to taste. Add shrimp and heat gently. Season with salt and pepper. Serve over grits. Top with grated sharp Cheddar cheese (optional).

SERVES 6.

CARROT, ZUCCHINI, AND APPLE MUFFINS

2 cups all-purpose flour
2 cups grated carrots
1 cup sugar
1 cup grated zucchini
1 golden Delicious apple, cored and finely chopped
¾ cup golden raisins
¾ cup coconut
½ cup almonds, coarsely chopped
1 tablespoon cinnamon
2 teaspoons baking soda
2 teaspoons grated orange peel
1 teaspoon vanilla extract
½ teaspoon salt
3 eggs
1 cup oil

Preheat oven to 375°. Mix all ingredients, except eggs and oil in large bowl. Beat eggs and oil in another bowl. Stir in flour mixture. Spoon ¼ cup batter into each muffin cup. Bake for 25 minutes. Serve warm or at room temperature.
MAKES ABOUT 24 MUFFINS.

RUTLEDGE BISCUITS WITH HOT SHERRIED FRUIT

2 cups self-rising flour
1 cup buttermilk
⅓ cup shortening

Cut shortening into flour. Add buttermilk and mix well. Knead on floured surface. Pat to ¾ inch thickness. Cut with biscuit cutter. Place on greased baking pan. (Iron skillet is best). Bake in 450° oven for 10 minutes or until nicely browned.

Hot Sherried Fruit
1 tablespoon cornstarch
¼ cup water
1 15-ounce can each fruit (peaches/pineapple/pears)
½ cup light brown sugar
1 tablespoon cinnamon
1 teaspoon allspice (optional)
½ cup cream sherry (or to taste)

Mix cornstarch and water; set aside. Combine all ingredients (except cornstarch mixture) in a 2-quart pot. Heat, do not boil. Add liquor and then add the cornstarch mixture. Cook until thickened.
SERVES 6 TO 8.

THE SHAW HOUSE

613 Cypress Court • Georgetown, South Carolina 29440 • (803) 546-9663 • Mary and Joe Shaw

The first European settlement in what is now Georgetown County was an ill-fated Spanish colony established in 1526 near Winyah Bay on the Atlantic. Almost two centuries later, Northern Europeans made a new effort to settle the area, and they flourished here. Today's Georgetown can trace its roots to those English, Scottish, French Huguenot, and German immigrants.

The Shaw House is a two-story home in a serene natural setting that offers a spectacular view overlooking miles of marshland. The spacious guest rooms are filled with antiques, and your stay includes a delicious Southern home-cooked breakfast with fresh hot bread and your own pot of coffee.

The Shaw House is a special delight for bird watchers, who can explore the fascinating species of Willowbank Marsh. Georgetown's Historic District will also please explorers on the lookout for interesting antique and gift shops, museums and restaurants. Golf courses, tennis courts, and two marinas are nearby, and Georgetown is within easy drives of Myrtle Beach, Pawleys Island, and Charleston.

$\mathscr{B}$REAKFAST CASSEROLE

1 pound mild sausage
2 to 3 cups of bread cubes
1 cup grated Cheddar cheese
6 eggs

2 cups milk
1 teaspoon salt
1 teaspoon dry mustard

Brown sausage and drain. Place 2 or 3 cups of bread cubes in a 9x13-inch lightly greased pan and top with sausage. Sprinkle 1 cup of grated cheese over sausage. Pour egg mixture (eggs, milk, salt, and mustard). Pour over the sausage. Set in refrigerator overnight. Bake at 350° for 45 minutes.

SERVES 8.

Authors' Tip: If preferred, the refrigeration step may be eliminated.

$\mathscr{B}$ELGIAN WAFFLES

1 package active dry yeast
2 cups warm milk
4 eggs, separated
1 tablespoon vanilla extract

2½ cups all-purpose flour
½ teaspoon salt
1 tablespoon sugar
½ cup melted butter (1 stick)

Sprinkle yeast over warm milk and stir. Beat egg yolks and add to yeast and vanilla. Sift dry ingredients and add to yeast mixture. Stir in melted butter. Beat egg whites and fold into mixture. Let stand 45 minutes before pouring batter into waffle iron.

MAKES 8 WAFFLES.

Chef's Hint: These can be frozen and reheated in toaster.

VEGGIE ANGEL BISCUITS

2 packages active dry yeast
¼ cup warm water (110° to 115°)
5 cups self-rising flour
1 teaspoon baking soda

2 tablespoons sugar
1 cup butter (2 sticks) or
   shortening
2 cups V8 juice

Dissolve yeast in warm water and put aside. Mix flour, baking soda, and sugar. Add shortening and mix together. Add yeast and mix together. Add V8 juice and mix well. Roll on floured board and cut with heart-shaped biscuit cutter. Start in a cold oven. Bake at 450°.

MAKES 24 BISCUITS.

MONTGOMERY'S GROVE BED & BREAKFAST

408 Harlee Street • Marion, South Carolina 29571 • (803) 423-5220 • Rick and Coreen Roberts

This 1893 Victorian manor house is known for its dramatic hallway constructed with 14-foot arches built by shipmakers. Listed on the National Register of Historic Places, the house offers five guest rooms, each with fireplace, and is furnished with period antiques. The wraparound porches provide comfortable spots for relaxation, or you can enjoy a stroll through the property's five acres of century-old trees and gardens.

Marion—a quaint village with antique shops, boutiques, and restaurants—is located at the midway point between the Northeast and Florida, ten minutes from I-95. Known as "the pretty little town on the way to the beach," Marion is only 35 miles from the popular resort city of Myrtle Beach.

MONTGOMERY'S GROVE APPLE CITRUS CRISP

4 cups tart apples, sliced
¼ cup orange juice
1 cup sugar
¾ cup all-purpose flour, sifted
½ teaspoon cinnamon
¼ teaspoon nutmeg
⅛ teaspoon salt
⅓ cup butter
Light cream

Mound apples in buttered pie plate and cover with orange juice . In a separate bowl, combine sugar, flour, spices and salt; cut in butter until mixture is crumbly. Sprinkle over apples. Bake until apples are tender and topping is crisp. Bake at 375° for 45 minutes. Serve warm with cream.

SERVES 6.

Authors' Tip: Similar to apple cobbler, the crisp is delicious plain, with cream, or with a scoop of ice cream.

ℒAUREL HILL PLANTATION

P. O. Box 190 • 8913 N. Highway 17 • McClellanville, South Carolina 29458 • (803) 887-3708
• Jackie and Lee Morrison

ℐn 1989, the devastation of Hurricane Hugo included the destruction of the original Laurel Hill, an 1850s plantation house listed on the National Register of Historic Places. But the inn has been lovingly reconstructed to recapture the romance of the past, combined with all the conveniences of contemporary living. Nestled in a nook beside a picturesque tidal creek, the inn offers spectacular panoramic views of Cape Romain's salt marshes, island waterways, and the Atlantic Ocean from its wraparound porches.

Views of the landscape are part of the charm of each of four guest rooms, with private baths. The rooms are furnished with carefully selected primitives and antiques, reflecting the time-honored tradition of hospitality of South Carolina's low country. Your stay will include a full country breakfast served in the dining room or on the porch. (Jackie tells us that the Breakfast Casserole is known to turn even hard-core grits haters into instant converts.) After dining, you can go crabbing from the dock, fish in the pond, or simply prop up your feet and soak in the scenery and leisurely life style.

The area's most popular attraction is the Cape Romain National Wildlife Refuge, accessible by boat only. Boats to Bull Island leave Moore's Landing, ten miles south of McClellanville, at 9:00 a.m. and pick up at 4:00 p.m. For information, call (803) 928-3368. We hear it's a wild place!

$\mathscr{B}$REAKFAST CASSEROLE

2 pounds bulk sausage	5 eggs
1 cup raw grits, cooked	1½ cups milk
¼ cup butter or margarine (½ stick)	Salt and pepper to taste
2 cups sharp Cheddar cheese, grated	

Brown and drain sausage and crumble in bottom of 9x13-inch greased casserole. Cook grits according to package directions (stiff is better than runny). Add margarine and cheese to cooked grits. Beat eggs, milk, salt and pepper together and add to slightly cooled grits mixture. Pour over sausage in casserole. Bake at 350° for one hour.

SERVES 8.

Chef's Hint: Try mixing 1 package regular and 1 package hot sausage. The recipe can be made ahead and then frozen. The casserole can easily be halved.

SERENDIPITY, AN INN

407 71st Avenue North • Myrtle Beach, South Carolina 29572 • (803) 449-5266 or
(800) 762-3229 • The Johnsons

*T*his inn—a small, Spanish mission-style complex—puts you just 300 yards from one of the best beaches in North America. Guests may choose from queen-size units to a full suite, and each room is uniquely decorated to reflect a different period. Off the beaten path, Serendipity offers quiet nights and peaceful days. A continental breakfast is served in the friendly "Garden Room," a cheery, friendly spot for relaxing and socializing. You can relax in the inn's quiet garden on a quiet street or take the short stroll to the busy beach front. Amenities include an outside hot tub and heated pool, shuffleboard, ping pong, outdoor gas grill, and a private seating area complete with a soft bubbling fountain.

Myrtle Beach offers myriad activities including championship golf courses, tennis courts, the fine restaurants of Grand Street, amusements, and shopping. The many country music theaters and clubs in town provide plenty of chances to kick up your heels.

CARROT LOAF

3 cups all-purpose flour
2 teaspoons baking soda
2 teaspoons baking powder
½ teaspoon salt
1 teaspoon cinnamon
4 eggs
2 cups sugar

1½ cups corn oil
1 teaspoon vanilla extract
2 cups grated raw carrots
1 cup chopped walnuts
1 14-ounce can crushed
  pineapple

Preheat oven to 350°. In large bowl sift together flour, baking soda, baking powder, salt and cinnamon. In separate bowl beat together eggs and sugar until pale yellow. Beat in oil and vanilla. Stir in sifted ingredients. Fold in carrots, walnuts and pineapple. Butter and lightly flour a 10-inch bundt or loaf pan. Pour batter into prepared pan and bake for 1 hour and 10 minutes or until cake tester comes clean.

MAKES 1 LOAF.

BANANA BREAD

1 cup butter
2 cups sugar
6 bananas, mashed
4 eggs, beaten

2½ cups all-purpose flour
2 teaspoons baking soda
1 teaspoon salt
1 cup walnuts, chopped

Mix butter and sugar until fluffy. Add bananas and eggs and mix together. Sift dry ingredients 3 times and blend with banana mixture. Do not overmix. Add nuts and mix lightly. Pour into 2 greased 1-quart loaf pans and bake at 350° for 45 minutes to 1 hour. Test for doneness with wooden toothpick. Cool on a wire rack.

MAKES 2 LOAVES.

Chef's Note: This bread freezes well.

$\mathscr{S}$WEET ANNIE'S BED, BREAKFAST & BARN

7201 Crow Cut Road, S. W. • Fairview, Tennessee 37062 • (615) 799-8833 • Ann and Charles Murphy

$\mathscr{U}$nlike most B&Bs, this contemporary home—located in a small town in the rural countryside of Williamson County—is furnished in modern style and features lots of windows, pastel colors, and peace and quiet. When the weather permits, breakfast is served on the upper section of a two-tiered deck overlooking the gardens and horse pastures. Other times, you will breakfast in the dining room. But prepare to be casual. The Murphys say that guests often gather in the kitchen, "which we love." Over breakfast, ask Ann and Charles about the 800-acre nature park which was given to Fairview at the death of one of the town's most interesting citizens.

Accommodations are light and airy. You can enjoy morning coffee in your room, or sit in the great room and take in the pastoral view through its large windows. The B&B offers a swimming pool and hot tub. Hiking is always popular, and the Murphys also have horses and bikes for riding. The Fairview

Nature Trail has marked riding and hiking trails, and the historic Natchez Trace also beckons.

Sweet Annie's is just a short drive south of Nashville with its cultural and historic sites, including the home of President Andrew Jackson, and a wealth of music, music, music. There's a golf course near the B&B, and many Tennessee and Kentucky lakes are within easy driving distance.

CINNAMON, RAISIN, CREAM CHEESE, BANANA FRENCH TOAST

Cinnamon raisin bread
Cream cheese
Bananas, sliced
Lemon juice
Eggs
Milk

Vanilla-butternut flavoring
Cinnamon
Nutmeg
Orange liqueur sauce (recipe follows)

For *each* serving take 2 pieces of cinnamon raisin bread. Spread one slice with cream cheese and a layer of sliced bananas which have been dipped in lemon juice. Put together like a sandwich. In a bowl, combine the egg, milk, and flavorings to taste. Dip each sandwich in the egg mixture. Grill until golden and serve with orange liqueur sauce. Garnish with an orange slice.

SERVES 1.

ORANGE LIQUEUR SAUCE

Mix 1 cup orange juice, ⅓ cup sugar, and 2 tablespoons of any orange liqueur. In a saucepan cook over medium heat until slightly thickened.

Chef's Hint: Make the sauce in double batches and keep one batch in the refrigerator for later use. The French toast may also be served with maple syrup.

Authors' Tip: If a non-alcoholic orange sauce is desired, substitute orange extract for the liqueur.

STRAWBERRY BREAKFAST PUDDING

½ cup toasted wheat germ,
  divided
1 cup nonfat vanilla yogurt
1 cup egg substitute

¼ cup honey
¼ cup unbleached flour
¼ teaspoon freshly grated nutmeg
2 cups sliced strawberries

Lightly coat a 1½-quart straight-sided casserole or baking dish with non-stick spray. Dust evenly with ¼ cup wheat germ. In a medium bowl, whisk yogurt briefly until smooth. Add the egg substitute, honey, flour, nutmeg, and remaining ¼ cup of wheat germ. Mix well.

Place strawberries in the bottom of the dish. Add the batter and place on the top shelf of the oven. Bake at 400° for 30 to 35 minutes or until the top is golden brown and a cake tester inserted in the middle comes clean. Serve warm or cold.

SERVES 4.

APPLE CRANBERRY CASSEROLE

Casserole
8 cups sliced red Delicious apples
1 bag (12 ounces) cranberries
½ cup brown sugar, lightly
  packed
½ cup white sugar

Topping
2 cups quick oatmeal
¾ to 1 cup brown sugar, lightly
  packed
¾ chopped pecans
½ cup margarine, melted

Combine the apples, cranberries, brown and white sugars, and put mixture in a large lightly greased casserole dish. Mix together the oatmeal, brown sugar, and pecans. Add the melted margarine and stir until mixed. Spread over fruit mixture and bake uncovered in a 350° oven for 45 minutes.

SERVES 8.

Chef's Note: One can of cranberry sauce with whole berries may be substituted for the fresh cranberries and sugar.

OLDE ENGLISH TUDOR INN BED & BREAKFAST

135 West Holly Ridge Road • Gatlinburg, Tennessee 37738 • (615) 436-7760 or (800) 541-3798
• Larry, Kathy and Willie Schuh

*T*his inn is set on a hillside in downtown Gatlinburg, just a short walk from many restaurants, shops, and attractions. Each of the seven charming guest rooms includes private bath and modern amenities. On crisp evenings, you can gather round the wood-burning stove in the large common room. There's also a secluded rear patio, award-winning garden with a four-level waterfall, and beautiful views of Great Smoky Mountain National Park.

A stay at the Olde English Tudor Inn includes a generous mountain breakfast served in the dining room or on the patio. Delectable breakfast dishes may include fresh fruit, pancakes or French toast, eggs, bacon, sausage, ham, and freshly baked bread.

Gatlinburg is a city that caters to its visitors with museums, restaurants, miniature golf, ski lift, and skiing. A few minutes driving will take you to Dolly Parton's entertainment park, Dollywood, horseback riding, rafting and swimming, hiking, fishing and the attractions of the Great Smokies.

GRANDMA'S WHITE BREAD

1 package active dry yeast
¼ cup warm water (105° to 115°)
2 cups milk, scalded
2 tablespoons sugar
2 teaspoons salt

1 tablespoon shortening
6¼ to 6½ cups sifted all-purpose flour

Soften yeast in warm water. Combine hot milk, sugar, salt, and shortening. Cool to lukewarm. Stir in 2 cups flour and beat well. Add yeast and mix. Add enough flour to make a moderately stiff dough. Knead on a lightly floured surface until smooth (about 8 minutes). Shape in a ball and place in a bowl that has been rubbed with margarine (turn over to "grease" entire surface). Cover with towel and let rise until double in size, about 1 hour. Punch down.

Preheat oven to 350°. Cut dough in half. Shape in 2 smooth balls, cover and let rest 10 minutes. Shape in loaves. Place dough in 2 greased (margarine) 1-quart loaf pans and cover. Let rise until doubled in size, about 1 hour. Bake in oven about 20 minutes until done.

MAKES 2 LOAVES.

Chef's Hint: After shaping the dough into loaves, the dough may be frozen in an airtight bag until ready for use. Place a in greased loaf pan and cover. Let rise overnight.

Apple Cornmeal Pancakes

⅔ cup cornmeal
½ cup sugar
1⅓ cups all-purpose flour
2 teaspoons baking powder
½ teaspoon salt
½ teaspoon allspice
2 large tart apples, peeled, cored, and shredded

3 eggs, beaten
1½ cups buttermilk
4 tablespoons vegetable oil, plus a small amount for cooking
Maple syrup

In a large bowl, mix together the corn meal, sugar, flour, baking powder, salt, and allspice. In a separate bowl, mix together the apples, eggs, buttermilk, and vegetable oil. Combine the dry ingredients into the wet ingredients. Cook on a greased hot grill until bubbles appear. Turn over and finish cooking. Serve with hot maple syrup.

SERVES 8 TO 10.

Carrot Cake

2 cups all-purpose flour
2 teaspoons ground cinnamon
1 teaspoon baking powder
¼ teaspoon salt
⅔ cup butter, softened
1 cup sugar

3 large eggs
⅔ cup milk
3 medium carrots, grated
½ cup chopped walnuts or ½ cup raisins (optional)

Mix together flour, cinnamon, baking powder, and salt. Beat together butter and sugar at medium speed until light and fluffy. Add eggs and beat well. At low speed, alternately beat flour mixture and milk into butter mixture. Stir in carrots and walnuts and pour into a greased and floured 1-quart loaf pan. Bake in a 350° oven for 40 to 50 minutes. Cool on a wire rack about 15 minutes. Turn out on rack and cool 30 minutes before cutting.

SERVES 12.

PPLE DELIGHT

Fruit mixture
- 5 large red Delicious apples, diced
- 1 large bunch of seedless grapes
- 1 20-ounce can pineapple tidbits, drained (save juice)
- 1 small bag mini-marshmallows
- 2 cups chopped walnuts (optional)

Sauce
- 2 tablespoons flour
- ½ cup sugar
- 1 egg, lightly beaten
- 2 tablespoons margarine
  Reserved pineapple juice (1 cup)

In a large bowl mix together the apples, grapes, pineapple tidbits, marshmallows, and walnuts. In a saucepan, combine the flour, sugar, egg, margarine, and pineapple juice. Cook on medium heat until thick. Cool thoroughly and add to the fruit mixture. Mix well and serve.

SERVES 6.

GRANDMA'S HOUSE BED & BREAKFAST

734 Pollard Road • P. O. Box 445 • Kodak, Tennessee 37764 • (615) 933-3512 or (800) 676-3512
• Hilda Hickman

At Grandma's House, you will enjoy the special hospitality native to East Tennessee. This tranquil B&B offers guest rooms named for Hilda's and her husband's grandmothers—Bonnie Telitha, Hassie Della and Melinda Evelyn. Each room has a private bath, and the cozy country decor includes Hilda's handmade quilts, crafts, and paintings. After a busy day in the Great Smoky Mountains National Park or nearby Gatlinburg, you can "come home" for a little R&R on the balcony or the swing on the big front porch. The inn also has two common rooms with television/VCR, games, and plenty of books and magazines. When the weather is warm, you can enjoy your full farm-style breakfast in the great outdoors.

In addition to the park and Gatlinburg, activities close at hand include historic sites, factory outlet shopping, horseback riding, caverns, museums, arts and crafts, golf courses, and amusement parks. Oak Ridge, Knoxville, and Jonesborough, Tennessee's oldest town, are located between 30 to 60 minutes' drive from Grandma's House.

PORK IN MILK GRAVY

2 pound pork tenderloin cut
  ¾-inch thick
  All-purpose flour for dredging

Salt and pepper to taste
2 tablespoons butter or margarine
2 cups milk

Trim excess fat from tenderloin. Dredge tenderloin with flour. Season with salt and pepper. Brown in butter at 350° in electric skillet. Reduce temperature to 225°; cover skillet. Cook for 30 minutes to 1 hour or until pork is tender. Add milk. Heat uncovered until bubbling hot. Serve immediately.

SERVES 6 TO 8.

$\mathscr{S}$NAPP INN BED & BREAKFAST

1990 Davy Crockett Park Road • Limestone, Tennessee 37681 • (423) 257-2482 • Dan and Ruth Dorgan

$\mathscr{T}$his 1815 Federal brick home invites you to experience country living in a friendly, family atmosphere. The antique-furnished home offers two guest rooms with private baths. You can simply relax and enjoy the scenic views of mountains and creek. Or shoot a "hot" game of pool or watch TV in the commons area.

Limestone is located in northeastern Tennessee, where the first settlements on the western side of the Appalachian mountains were located. Legendary residents of the area included Daniel Boone, Davy Crockett, John Sevier, and Presidents Andrew Jackson and Andrew Johnson. From the inn, you can walk to the Davy Crockett Birthplace State Park with its large swimming pool. You might also plan a short drive to visit Andrew Johnson's home in Greeneville or to visit Jonesborough. Just 15 minutes' drive from the inn, Jonesborough was founded in 1779 and is Tennessee's oldest town. Today, it is a living restored community offering a fascinating glimpse into history. A walking tour of the Historic District includes 29 structures dating from the early 1800s.

CHEESE GRITS CASSEROLE

4 cups water
1 teaspoon salt
1 cup quick grits
1½ cup grated sharp Cheddar
  cheese, divided

½ cup butter or margarine
  (1 stick)
4 eggs, lightly beaten
1 cup milk
¼ teaspoon cayenne pepper

Preheat oven to 350°. Grease a 2-quart baking dish. Bring water and salt to a boil in a large saucepan. Slowly stir in grits. Cover, reduce heat, and cook 5 minutes, stirring occasionally. Remove from heat. Stir in 1 cup of cheese and butter until melted. Add eggs, milk, and pepper. Blend well. Pour mixture into prepared dish. Sprinkle with remaining ½ cup cheese. Bake 45 to 60 minutes or until cheese is golden brown. Cool 10 minutes before serving.

MAKES 6-8 SERVINGS.

BREAKFAST PIE

1 pound sausage, cooked and
  crumbled
6 eggs, beaten

2 cups shredded Cheddar cheese
1 can packaged crescent rolls (8)

In a medium bowl combine the sausage, eggs, and Cheddar cheese. Line the bottom of a pie pan with 4 crescent rolls. Cover with the egg mixture and top with the 4 remaining crescent rolls. Bake at 350° for 30 minutes.

SERVES 6.

SOUR CREAM PIE

1½ cups raisins
1½ cups sugar
3 egg yolks, lightly beaten
1½ tablespoons flour
1½ cups sour cream
½ teaspoons ground cloves

1 teaspoon nutmeg
1 baked pie crust
Meringue
3 egg whites
1 tablespoon sugar

Prepare the pie. In a medium saucepan, boil the raisins in just enough water to cover and set aside to soak. In a small bowl mix the sugar, egg yolks, flour, sour cream, cloves, and nutmeg. Add the mixture to the raisins and cook until thick. Pour mixture into a baked pie crust.

To prepare the meringue, beat the 3 egg whites until stiff, adding 1 tablespoon of sugar while beating. Cover the top of the pie with meringue and bake at 325° for 3 to 5 minutes or until light brown.

SERVES 8.

$\mathcal{F}$ALL CREEK FALLS BED & BREAKFAST INN

Route 3, Box 298-B • Pikeville, Tennessee 37367 • (423) 881-5494 • Doug and Rita Pruett

$\mathcal{T}$his country manor house, located a mile from the beautiful Fall Creek Falls State Resort Park, is distinguished by its friendly, country Victorian ambiance. In an unusual touch, you will be give a key to your room and the house when you arrive. The inn offers eight air-conditioned bedrooms, individually decorated. Chef Doug's gourmet breakfasts are served in the elegant dining room at tables set with fine china, silver and crystal. Six different breakfasts are available, one each day, and may include such delicious selections as pecan waffles with homemade apple cider syrup and eggs Benedict.

The area's number one attraction is the park. Rated tops in the state, it attracts more than 900,000 visitors annually. The spectacular 256-foot Fall Creek Falls is the highest waterfall east of the Rockies—90 feet higher than Niagara Falls. The park's 20,000 acres encompass more waterfalls, rocky cliffs, and natural woods, making it one of the most scenic parks in the nation.

The area offers many recreational choices including camping and hiking, and for the hardy, there is rock climbing and rappelling. The challenging golf course is rated one of the nation's Top 10 public courses. At Fall Creek Lake, you can rent canoes, pedal boats, and fishing boats. There are also nature trails, bike trails, and equestrian trails, an Olympic-size pool and wading pools, tennis courts, ball fields, horseshoe pits, and basketball courts. The park's wildly beautiful environment made it the perfect setting for the film *The Jungle Book*.

BREAKFAST TORTILLAS

½ pound sausage
8 eggs (beaten)
½ cup shredded Cheddar cheese
8 tortillas

½ cup mushrooms, sautéed (optional)
Salsa or picante sauce (optional)

In a skillet cook the sausage and pour off the fat. Combine eggs into sausage and cook until softly done. Sprinkle in the cheese. Place a portion onto each tortilla, fold once; fold each end and roll. Serve with salsa or picante sauce.

SERVES 4.

Chef's Hint: Try substituting sautéed green bell peppers, chopped ham, or crumbled bacon for the sausage.

Authors' Note: Easy and fun to eat! Olé!

SCRUMPTIOUS STRAWBERRY BREAD

3 cups all-purpose flour
1 teaspoon soda
1 teaspoon salt
1 teaspoon cinnamon
2 cups sugar

4 eggs, well beaten
2 10-ounce packages frozen
   strawberries, drained (reserve
   for sauce)
1¼ cups oil

In a large bowl mix together the flour, soda, salt, cinnamon, and sugar. Mix by and and place dough in two greased and floured loaf pans. Bake at 350° for 1 hour.

MAKES 2 LOAVES.

Chef's Hint: For a delectable sauce, mix the reserved strawberry juice with 1 8-ounce package cream cheese. Add just enough sugar to sweeten and whip all together in a blender.

SUPER BREAKFAST CASSEROLE

4 frozen hash brown patties
1 pound sausage or bacon,
   cooked, drained, and crumbled

6 eggs, lightly beaten
1 cup milk
6 ounces grated Cheddar cheese

Line an 8x8-inch baking dish with frozen hash brown patties. Sprinkle hash browns with sausage or bacon. Mix together the eggs and milk and pour over the meat and has brown patties. Top with grated cheese. This dish is best if prepared ahead and refrigerated overnight. Bake at 350° for 45 minutes to 1 hour.

MAKES 4 TO 6 SERVINGS.

$\mathcal{P}$ICKETT'S HARBOR

P. O. Box 97AA • Cape Charles, Virginia 23310 • (804) 331-2212 • Sara and Cooke Coffigon

$\mathcal{A}$t the southernmost tip of the Delmarva Peninsula on Virginia's Eastern Shore stands an inn built in 1976 but designed in eighteenth-century style. Pickett's Harbor features floors, cupboards, and doors fashioned of rafters from an eignteenth-century James River barn. Family heirlooms and antiques fill its rooms. Outside, the inn is surrounded by loblolly pines, cedars, and hollies, and the backyard with its tiny sand dunes leads to the inn's wide private beach on Chesapeake Bay.

Wherever your breakfast is served—on the porch, in the kitchen or the dining room—you will be treated to a view of the shimmering bay. Your full country breakfast will include Sara's stand-out homemade jellies and jams.

SPARAGUS QUICHE

15 spears fresh asparagus or
    1 15-ounce can asparagus
 5 eggs
 1 cup skim or 2% milk
 1 tablespoon chopped fresh basil
 ½ teaspoon salt

1 tablespoon chopped spring
  onions
1 cup grated sharp Cheddar
  cheese
1 cup chopped red bell pepper

Spray a 9- or 10-inch glass pie plate with cooking oil spray. After breaking off the tough ends of the asparagus spears, steam for five minutes. Place asparagus in bottom of the pie plate. Beat eggs, milk, basil, salt, and spring onions, and pour over the asparagus. Top with grated cheese and red peppers. Refrigerate overnight. Bake at 350° for 30 minutes. Allow quiche to cool for 15 minutes before serving.

SERVES 8.

Chef's Note: This is a good, low-calorie quiche.

HAT A PANCAKE

4 tablespoons margarine
1 cup all-purpose flour
4 eggs, lightly beaten

1 cup milk
Powdered sugar
Fruit topping or maple syrup

Preheat oven to 400°. In a 10-inch ovenproof skillet melt the margarine. In a medium bowl mix the flour, eggs, and milk. Ignore the lumps; do not beat until smooth. Pour batter into the heated skillet with smoking butter and bake at 400° for 20 minutes. Do not open the oven door.

After 20 minutes remove from the oven and sprinkle pancake with powdered sugar. Return to the oven for 10 minutes. Serve hot, after slicing the pancake into 6 wedges. Top with fruit topping or syrup.

SERVES 6.

Authors' Tip: To cut down on egg yolks, try using two whole eggs plus four egg whites. You can also try using half margarine and half canola oil. If a lighter pancake is preferred, substitute self-rising flour for the plain flour.

$\mathscr{S}$WEET POTATO BISCUITS

2 cups fully cooked mashed
　sweet potatoes
½ cup vegetable shortening
¾ cup sugar

3 cups sifted all-purpose flour
7 teaspoons baking powder
1 teaspoon salt
　Melted butter

Place hot mashed sweet potatoes in a bowl with the shortening and sugar. Stir to dissolve. Sift the flour, baking powder, and salt, and add to the potato mixture. On a floured board roll or pat to 1 half-inch thick. Cut with a biscuit cutter. Brush tops lightly with butter and bake at 350° for 20 to 25 minutes.

MAKES ABOUT 34 BISCUITS.

Chef's Hint: Good with Virginia ham.

BLUE KNOLL FARM

Route 1, Box 141 • Castleton, Virginia 22716 • (540) 937-5234 • Mary and Gil Carlson

Situated in a scenic valley at the foot of Castleton Mountain, this 19th century farmhouse was constructed before the Civil War, with an expansion added just after the turn of the century. Although Blue Knoll is only 65 miles west of Washington, D. C., the hurly-burly of city life seems centuries away. The inn sits beside a quiet country lane, amid rolling fields where cattle graze and wild flowers bloom.

For breakfast, tables in the dining room are set with crisp linen placemats and napkins, family china and sterling, and fresh flowers. Enjoy delicious breads or muffins, strata, quiche or egg casseroles, mixed with lively conversation is this charming setting.

For delightful excursions, the Blue Ridge Mountains, Shenandoah National Park and Skyline Drive, as well as colonial villages, antique shops and wineries are all nearby.

ℬLUE KNOLL CHEESY CREAMED EGGS

3 tablespoons butter or margarine
2 tablespoons all-purpose flour
1 cup milk
  Pepper
½ cup shredded medium or sharp
  Cheddar cheese

4 hard-boiled eggs, sliced
4 (or more) slices bacon, cooked
  and crumbled
  Toast points or cornbread sticks

In a sauté pan, prepare a white sauce by melting the butter or margarine until bubbly; then add the flour, mixing well. Gradually blend in the milk and pepper. Cook, stirring until the sauce thickens. Add the cheese and stir until melted and smooth. Add sliced eggs and crumbled bacon, mixing gently. Serve over toast points or freshly baked conrbread sticks or muffins.

SERVES 4, BUT RECIPE CAN EASILY BE DOUBLED.

𝒦EY LIME MUFFINS

2 cups sifted all-purpose flour
1 cup sugar
3 teaspoons baking powder
½ teaspoon salt
¼ cup milk

2 eggs, lightly beaten
¼ cup vegetable oil
1 teaspoon freshly grated lime
  peel
¼ cup freshly squeezed lime juice

Preheat oven to 400°. Into a large bowl, sift the flour, sugar, baking powder, and salt. In a medium bowl, combine remaining ingredients: milk, eggs, oil, peel, and juice. Add the liquid all at once to the flour mixture, stirring lightly with fork, only until moist. The batter will be somewhat lumpy. Spoon the batter into greased muffin cups. Bake for 15 to 20 minutes. Remove the muffins from the pan to a wire rack.

MAKES 12 MUFFINS.

Chef's Hint: During warm weather these light muffins are a favorite. They are delicious served warm with butter and/or orange or lime marmalade.

BRANDY (OR RUM) APPLESAUCE BREAD

1 cup raisins
½ cup plus 1 tablespoon brandy
  (or rum)
½ cup shortening
1 cup sugar
1 egg, beaten
2 cups all-purpose flour, divided
1 teaspoon baking soda

1 teaspoon salt
1 teaspoon cinnamon
½ teaspoon nutmeg
¼ teaspoon allspice
¼ teaspoon ground cloves
1 cup applesauce
1 cup chopped pecans

In a small bowl, combine the raisins and the brandy or rum; cover and refrigerate several hours or overnight.

Grease a 9x5x3-inch loaf pan. Preheat oven to 350°. In a bowl, cream the shortening and sugar. Add the egg, mixing well. Combine 1⅔ cups flour, soda, salt, and spices; add to the creamed mixture alternately with applesauce—beginning and ending with the flour mixture.

Drain the raisins and dredge the pecans and raisins in the remaining ⅓ cup flour, stirring to coat well. Fold into the batter. Spoon batter into the prepared pan. Bake for approximately 1 hour and 15 minutes. Check at the end of 1 hour. When bread is done and tester comes clean, let it cool in the pan. Store in the refrigerator or freeze for future use.

Chef's Note: This is a good wintertime bread. This recipe appeared in *Southern Living* magazine.

MAKES 1 LOAF.

Authors' Note: This is a heavy, dark bread with a wonderful aroma.

THE OAKS BED & BREAKFAST INN

311 East Main Street • Christiansburg, Virginia 24073 • (540) 381-1500 • Margaret and Tom Ray

This elegant and historic B&B, built circa 1889, has been featured in many national magazines. It easy to see why. The Oaks seems made for gracious relaxation. The wraparound porch with its Kennedy rockers and wicker furniture invites you to sit and while away the time. The perennial garden, complete with fountain and fish pond, is a popular spot for breakfast and tea. Three Queen Anne tables in the dining room seat 14 for breakfast, which is served on china and sterling under the glow of candlelight. The ambiance is enhanced with music from the sound system cleverly housed in a rare old Flemish bookcase.

Guests at The Oaks have included ambassadors, admirals, generals, and close friends of President and Mrs. Clinton. Margaret reports that one of her most interesting visitors was Baron Stig Ramal, president of the Nobel Foundation in Stockholm. "But the best by far," Margaret says, "are the fantastic folks . . . just plain folks . . . who have visited us from 48 states and 20 foreign countries."

The inn is located near the Blue Ridge Parkway and the Appalachian Trail, and the area offers an abundance of activities including caverns, craft shops, outdoor theater and a local winery. The annual Victorian Christmas at The Oaks makes December a very special time to visit.

*L*EMON BROCCOLI QUICHE

1 unbaked 9-inch pastry shell
1 10-ounce package frozen broccoli cuts (or fresh broccoli)
1 8-ounce can sliced water chestnuts, drained
¾ cup mayonnaise
¾ cup half and half
3 eggs, slightly beaten
⅛ teaspoon nutmeg

2 tablespoons freshly squeezed lemon juice
¼ teaspoon soy sauce
Salt, to taste
2 teaspoons cornstarch
1½ cups shredded Swiss cheese
Red pepper flakes
Paprika

Steam the broccoli and set aside. (Make sure all the pieces are medium size and uniform.) Preheat oven to 350°. Combine the broccoli with the water chestnuts and set aside. Mix together the remaining ingredients, except the cheese. Place the broccoli, water chestnuts, and cheese evenly into the crust. Carefully pour the egg mixture into the crust. Sprinkle with paprika. Bake for 35 to 40 minutes or until set. Let stand 15 minutes before serving.

SERVES 8.

Chef's Note: This quiche is excellent—great texture, great lemony taste. Serve it right from the oven. It loses its good texture if served hours later, and never make it the night before.

APPLE STRUDEL MUFFINS

2 cups sifted all-purpose flour
½ cup firmly packed light brown sugar
3 teaspoons baking powder
1 teaspoon salt
½ cup butter (1 stick)

1 or 2 apples, peeled and diced
1 egg
⅔ cup milk
¼ cup chopped nuts
1 tablespoon white sugar

In a large bowl, mix together the flour, sugar, baking powder salt, and butter, working the butter into the flour with a pastry blender until coarse crumbs form. Remove ½ cup for topping.

Add the apples, egg, and milk to the flour mixture and blend just until smooth. Spoon into oiled muffin tins.

Add the chopped nuts and 1 tablespoon sugar to the ½ cup flour mixture and set aside. Sprinkle evenly on the muffins. Bake at 425° for approximately 20 minutes.

MAKES 12 MUFFINS.

Chef's Hint: This is a basic muffin recipe we use to make many variations. Mix flours, i.e., whole-wheat, oat bran, white. Use an egg substitute for whole eggs if desired. Substitute fruit juice for milk. Add raisins or nuts to the batter. Other fun combinations include using fresh chopped cranberries instead of apples, adding 1 tablespoon grated orange peel, substituting orange juice for the milk, or substituting fresh blueberries for the apples. Another possibility is to use chopped firm pears and 1 tablespoon lemon juice. Pears taste great with nutmeg. Serve with honey butter. Still another variation is to soak dried apricots in boiling water, drain, and chop. Combine with chopped dates and nuts for Christmas muffins.

BERRIES–THREE OAT MOUSSE

Oat Mousse

3 tablespoons regular or quick-cook rolled oats

1¼ cups milk

1 tablespoon sugar

1 tablespoon of B&B liqueur or Grand Marnier or Raspberry Chambord

2 tablespoons water

1 tablespoon unflavored gelatin

½ cup plain yogurt

1½ cups whipping cream (chill bowl and beaters in freezer)

In a saucepan simmer oats and milk for several minutes, stirring constantly. Stir in the sugar and remove from the heat. Cool, then add the liqueur. Set aside. In a small bowl place the water and sprinkle the gelatin on top. Stir until gelatin is dissolved. Cool, then add to the oat mixture. Add the yogurt and whisk until mixed. Whip the cream until stiff and fold into oat mixture. Pour into a ring mold and chill for several hours or overnight.

Unmold on a pretty crystal platter. Carefully pour the Raspberry Sauce (recipe follows) around edge. Fill the center of mold with strawberries, raspberries, and blueberries and decorate the outside edge with berries. Be as artistic as you want to be, i.e., strawberry fans or red rosebuds. Pour Raspberry Sauce on fruit in center. SERVES 8 TO 10.

Chef's Hint: This elegant dish is simple to make and wonderful for late breakfast, brunch, a light and lovely dessert for any special occasion. The Raspberry Sauce is perfectly wonderful on ice cream or French toast.

Raspberry Sauce

1 package frozen raspberries

1 tablespoon red currant jelly

1 teaspoon grated orange peel

2 tablespoons the same liqueur used in the mousse

Strawberries, red raspberries, and blueberries for garnish

Make the sauce. Thaw the raspberries and bring to a boil in a saucepan. Strain through a fine sieve, and using a wooden spoon, press as much pulp through as possible, retaining the seeds in sieve. Scrape the pulp with a spatula and combine with the juice. Return the raspberries to the saucepan. Add the currant jelly and the orange peel. Bring to low boil for 2 to 3 minutes. Cool partially and add the liqueur. When cool, chill in the refrigerator.

OAK GROVE PLANTATION

P. O. Box 45 • Cluster Springs, Virginia 24535 • (804) 575-7137 • Mary Pickett Craddock

*O*ak Grove has been the family home of the Easleys and Craddocks since 1820. And "family" is the watchword at this handsome antebellum B&B. The recipe for Aunt Bell's Rocks included here is a delicious way to sample Pickett's family history: "A family recipe handed down to my mother and then to me, it's my favorite cookie recipe in the whole world! In an antique family diary, I found a record of my great-aunt making it in 1917."

Open from May to September, the inn offers a special three-night midweek package for families. Pickett, who is a pre-school teacher, organizes morning and afternoon activities for her young guests so parents can enjoy time on their own.

The guest rooms at Oak Grove include fireplaces and are furnished with comfortable period furniture and family pieces. A full country breakfast is served in the Victorian dining room. Afterwards you catch a nap, read, or listen to music in the elegant parlor or on the cheerful sun porch.

The plantation includes 400 acres where you can hike or bike on rustic farm roads and paths. A variety of historic sites and recreational activities are available nearby.

Spinach Crustless Quiche

2 cups grated white Cheddar cheese
2 10-ounce packages frozen chopped spinach (thawed and squeezed dry)
9 eggs, beaten slightly

1 pound cottage cheese
½ pound cubed Feta cheese
1 teaspoon nutmeg
¼ cup unseasoned breadcrumbs (for dusting the baking pan)
Cooking oil spray

Preheat oven to 350°. Set aside ¼ cup of the Cheddar cheese. In a large bowl mix spinach thoroughly with the eggs, cottage cheese, 1¾ cups Cheddar cheese, Feta cheese, and nutmeg. Spray a 13x9-inch baking pan thoroughly with cooking spray. Dust the bottom of the pan with breadcrumbs. Spread the spinach mixture evenly in the pan. Sprinkle the top with ¼ cup Cheddar cheese. Bake for 50 minutes to an hour until golden and firm to the touch.
SERVES 10.

Asparagus Crustless Quiche

10 eggs
½ cup all-purpose flour
1 teaspoon baking powder
1 teaspoon salt
2 cups cottage cheese
4 cups shredded white Cheddar cheese

½ cup melted butter or margarine (1 stick)
1 pound asparagus, washed, tough ends broken off, and cut into 1-inch pieces
Paprika

In a large bowl beat the eggs until light. Add the flour, baking powder, salt, cottage cheese, Cheddar cheese, butter, and asparagus. Mix well. Pour into a buttered 13x9-inch pan. Sprinkle paprika on top. Bake at 350° for 35 to 40 minutes. Cut into squares.
SERVES 10.

Authors' Tip: For a healthier alternative, use egg substitute for part or all of the eggs. Using low-fat sharp cheese and 1 percent cottage cheese also helps reduce the fat content.

ALLY LUNN BREAD

1 package active dry yeast	6 tablespoons butter or margarine
½ cup warm water (110° to 115°)	½ teaspoon salt
2 tablespoons sugar	2 well-beaten eggs
½ cup milk	2 cups all-purpose flour

In a small bowl mix together the yeast, warm water, and sugar. Let stand 10 minutes or until foamy.

In a saucepan, scald the milk and add the butter or margarine and salt. Cool to room temperature. Beat the eggs in the food processor. Add the cool milk and shortening. Add the yeast and flour gradually to the above mixture. Process until smooth. Let rise in the food processor until doubled in bulk (about 20 minutes). Pour into a greased bundt mold. Let rise again about an hour. (It will be a soft dough). Bake at 425° for about 20 minutes, until lightly brown.

MAKES 1 BUNDT LOAF.

AUNT BELL'S ROCKS

2 cups light brown sugar	½ teaspoon ground cloves
1 cup margarine	1 teaspoon cinnamon
3 eggs, well beaten	1 cup walnuts
1¾ cups whole-wheat flour	1 15-opunce box seedless raisins
1¾ cups unbleached flour	1 teaspoon soda (dissolved in 3
½ teaspoon salt	tablespoons hot water)
½ teaspoon nutmeg	

In a bowl, cream the sugar and margarine. Add the well-beaten eggs, flour and spices, nuts and raisins. Last, add soda in hot water. Drop from a spoon onto greased cookie sheet. Cook for 10 minutes at 350°.

MAKES 36 COOKIES.

Chef's Hint: The cookies store best with an apple slice in a tight container.

THE BAILIWICK INN

4023 Chain Bridge Road • Fairfax, Virginia 22030 • (703) 691-2266 or (800) 366-7666 • Ann and Ray Smith

The "house across from the Courthouse" was built by Joshua Gunnel in the 19th century and is an important landmark in Fairfax, a town on the National Historic Register. The house was purchased by the Smiths in 1989. To complete their painstaking renovation, they worked with a group of six decorators, assisted by the staff of the Fairfax County Library's Virginia Room. The inn includes 14 bedrooms, with baths. Each room is named for a Virginian and decorated in a style appropriate to its namesake. The front and back gardens have also been designed to reflect the house's original era.

The Smiths will be delighted to tell you about the inn's fascinating history.

Morning at the Bailiwick begins with the mouth-watering aromas of baking bread and roasting coffee. Your rates include both home-cooked breakfast and afternoon tea. You can treat yourself to a candlelight dinner by advance reservation.

Fairfax is an easy 20-minute Metrorail ride from Washington, D.C. Other nearby attractions include the Manassas Civil War Park and the rolling hills, small towns and vineyards of Virginia's horse country to the west.

BREAKFAST VOL-AU-VENT

1 pound pork sausage (hot or
   medium)
1½ tablespoons butter
1 medium onion, chopped
1 cup chopped celery
4 ounces mushrooms, sliced
1½ tablespoons all-purpose flour
1 10¾-ounce can cream of
   mushroom soup

1 tablespoon chopped pimento
1 cup milk
   Salt and pepper
8 hard boiled eggs
8 puff pastry shells
   Slices of tomato and parsley
   sprigs for garnish

Cook, crumble, and drain the sausage, then set aside. In a saucepan, melt the butter and sauté the onion, celery, and mushrooms. Add the flour and cook for 1 minute. Add the sausage, mushrooms, soup, pimento, and milk, stirring well over medium heat. Add salt and pepper to taste. Add the sliced eggs, stirring gently until mixture is heated through. Keep warm.

Bake 8 frozen pastry shells according to directions. Remove the tops and reserve. Scoop out the center. Place the warm, prepared pastry shells on plate. Spoon sausage-egg mixture into each pastry shell to overflowing. Replace pastry caps. Garnish with tomato slices and parsley sprigs. Serve immediately.
   SERVES 8.

REFRIGERATOR POTATO ROLLS

1½ cup warm water (105° to 115°)
2 packages active dry yeast
½ cup sugar
1 tablespoon salt
2 eggs

½ cup butter (1 stick)
½ cup warm, unseasoned mashed
   potatoes
6½ cups all-purpose flour
1 tablespoon melted butter

Pour warm water into a large bowl. Sprinkle the yeast over the water and add the sugar and salt. Stir with a wooden spoon until completely dissolved. Let stand a few minutes. Add the 2 eggs, butter, warm mashed potatoes, and 3 cups of flour. Beat until smooth. Add 2 cups flour, and blend with hands until the flour is incorporated.

Add the remaining 1½ cups of flour. Mix with hands until dough is smooth and stiff enough to leave sides of the bowl. Knead for 5 minutes on lightly floured counter until smooth and elastic. Add more flour as needed. Place in a lightly buttered bowl. Brush the top of the dough with melted butter and cover with waxed paper and a damp dish towel. Let rise in the refrigerator for 2 hours or until doubled in bulk.

Remove the waxed paper. Punch down and cover with new waxed paper and a damp towel, and refrigerate. Can be refrigerated up to one week. Keep towel damp.

About 2 hours before serving remove from refrigerator. Proof in a warm oven. Place a pan with ½-inch of boiling water in the bottom of the oven. Let rise for about 45 minutes. Form dough into rolls. Bake at 375° for 25 to 30 minutes.

MAKES 15 TO 20 ROLLS.

$\mathscr{C}$INNAMON ROLLS

Use half of the dough of the above Refrigerator Potato Rolls. Roll dough into an 18x9-inch rectangle. Spread with 2 tablespoons softened butter and sprinkle with ½ cup sugar mixed with 2 teaspoons cinnamon. Roll up tightly, beginning at the wide end. Seal well by pinching edges of roll together. Even up the roll by stretching slightly. Cut roll into 1¼-inch slices and place 15 of them into greased 13x9-inch pan, or cut 1-inch slices and place 18 of them in greased muffin cups. Cover and let rise until doubled in size (about 45 minutes).

Bake at 375° for 25 to 30 minutes. Frost while warm with Quick White Icing or follow Sticky Bun or Frosted Orange Rolls recipes.

MAKES 15 TO 18 ROLLS.

QUICK WHITE ICING

Sift 1 cup powdered sugar into a bowl. Moisten with cream or milk to spreading consistency. Add flavoring (e.g., vanilla extract). Spread over slightly warm breads.

MAKES ½ TO ¾ CUP ICING.

STICKY BUNS

½ cup butter (1 stick), melted
¾ cup firmly packed light brown sugar

1½ cup pecan halves
1½ tablespoons light corn syrup

Stir butter, brown sugar, pecans, and corn syrup with a fork in 13x9-inch baking pan. Follow the previous recipe for Cinnamon Rolls and put 15 in the prepared pan, on top of the caramel mixture, 5 rolls down and 3 rolls across. Let rise 45 minutes in a warm oven with a pan of ½-inch of boiling water in the bottom of the oven. Remove both the buns and the pan of water from the oven. Bake at 375° for 25 minutes until light brown. Place a cookie sheet on top of the pan upside down. Turn over immediately, leaving buns on the cookie sheet. Let sit for 5 minutes. Separate the buns with 2 forks to serve.

MAKES 15 BUNS.

FROSTED ORANGE ROLLS

Follow the above recipe for Cinnamon Rolls, except instead of using cinnamon, sugar, and butter, spread the dough with half of the Creamy Orange Frosting. Let rise. Bake, and remove from the pan. Spread with the remainder of the frosting.

CREAMY ORANGE FROSTING

3 tablespoons soft butter	2 tablespoons orange juice
1 tablespoon grated orange peel	1½ cups sifted powdered sugar

In a small bowl mix the butter, grated orange peel, orange juice, and powdered sugar until smooth.

MAKES 1 CUP FROSTING.

SCONES

3 cups all-purpose flour	1 teaspoon grated orange peel
1/3 cup sugar	1 cup buttermilk
2½ teaspoons baking powder	2 tablespoon sugar mixed with ¼
¾ teaspoon baking soda	teaspoon cinnamon
¾ teaspoon salt	Whipping cream
¾ cup butter (1½ sticks)	Fruit preserves
½ cup currants or chopped dates	

In a large bowl, stir together the flour, sugar, baking powder, soda, and salt. Cut the butter with pastry blender or two knives into the dry ingredients until coarse crumbs form. Stir in the fruit and orange peel. Make a well in the middle of the mixture and add the buttermilk all at once. Stir the mixture with a fork until the dough pulls away from the sides of the bowl. With your hands, gather the dough into a ball and turn out onto a lightly floured surface. Roll out into ½-inch thick circle. Using 1- to 1½-inch cutter, cut into individual scones. Place on a greased baking sheet 1½ inches apart. Sprinkle with the sugar/cinnamon mixture. Bake at 425° for 10 to 11 minutes until lightly browned. Serve warm with lightly whipped cream and a variety of fruit preserves.

MAKES ???? SCONES.

CALEDONIA FARM

Route 1, Box 2080 • Flint Hill, Virginia 22627 • (540) 675-3693 • Phil Irwin

The view of the Blue Ridge Mountains from this stone country home is simply magnificent. The Federal-style house and summer kitchen were completed in 1812, and you can still see the two-foot thick walls and 32-foot beams. Restored in 1965, the house also features its original mantels, paneled windows, and pine floors. Listed on the National Register of Historic Places, the manor house and summer kitchen are a Virginia Historic Landmark.

The B&B was christened Caledonia, a mythical name for Scotland, to honor the area's first immigrants. The open countryside, reminiscent of England and Ireland, remains virtually unspoiled today. Guests never forget its spectacular view of the Skyline Drive atop the Shenandoah National Park.

The charming and romantic inn includes two guest rooms and one suite—each with working fireplace, individual heat control and air conditioning. Breakfasts are served at hourly intervals and offer your choice of eggs Benedict, smoked salmon, custom omelets, and lots of extras.

The property is also a working cattle farm. Guests can enjoy bicycle rides, lawn games, and hay rides. Riding, canoeing, tennis and golf, caves, wineries, historic sites, antiques shopping, and superb dining are all close by. Don't want to miss your chance to drive the Skyline!

EGGS BENEDICT CALEDONIA

2 English muffins, split
   Butter or margarine
4 slices Canadian bacon or ham
4 eggs, poached

1 package Hollandaise sauce mix
3 tablespoons lemon juice
   Garnish of your choice

Toast or broil the muffin halves and spread with butter. Top with slices of the Canadian bacon or ham. Keep muffins warm in a 160° oven. Poach the eggs for 3½ minutes in cups sprayed with cooking oil spray. When the whites are set and the yolks are still liquid, place inverted eggs upon muffins. Prepare a Hollandaise sauce replacing the 3 tablespoons of water with lemon juice. Cover the eggs with the sauce. Garnish with fresh parsley, a kiwi slice, a strawberry half, or the favorite garnish of your choice.

SERVES 2.

Chef's Hint: Practice this dish for confidence!

APPLE NUT BREAD

2 cups all-purpose flour
¾ cup sugar
1 tablespoon baking powder
½ tablespoon baking soda
½ tablespoon ground cinnamon

1 egg, lightly beaten
2 tablespoons vegetable oil
1 cup applesauce
1 cup chopped nuts

In a large bowl combine the flour, sugar, baking powder, soda, and cinnamon. Add the egg, oil, and applesauce and blend well. Add the nuts. Pour the batter into a greased 5x9-inch loaf pan or a 12-cup muffin pan. Bake at 350° for 45 minutes. Test with a toothpick for doneness. Cool.

SERVES 12.

HUBARB GINGER SAUCE

3 cups chopped rhubarb
⅓ cup sugar
⅓ cup water

3 tablespoons finely chopped
   crystallized ginger
⅓ cup orange liqueur

In a medium saucepan, combine the rhubarb, sugar, and water. Bring to a boil and simmer uncovered, stirring often until the mixture reaches the consistency of applesauce. Stir in the ginger and liqueur and simmer another 15 minutes, adding water if mixture is too thick. Cool. Serve on pancakes, waffles, or most anything.

MAKES 1 CUP.

ORN STUFFING BAKE

¼ cup finely chopped celery
¼ cup finely chopped onion
½ tablespoon brown sugar
1 teaspoon Dijon mustard

½ teaspoon paprika
1 can (10 ounces) creamed corn
1½ cups cornbread stuffing

To prepare, in a medium bowl combine all ingredients. Blend well. Place in a 9-inch greased pie plate or 1½-quart dish. Bake at 400° for 30 minutes. Garnish.

SERVES 4.

Route 1, Box 306-A • Leesburg, Virginia 22075 • (703) 327-4325 • Carol and Bill Chamberlin

$\mathcal{B}$uilt in 1745, Fleetwood Farm was the home of a physician friend of Martha and George Washington. John Singleton Mosby, the famous "Gray Ghost," stayed at Fleetwood at least twice during the Civil War. Little wonder that this Loudoun County home is a Virginia Historic Landmark, listed on the National Register of Historic Places. The structure, which retains its original woodwork and flooring, was restored and rehabilitated over a 16-year period and opened as a B&B in 1988. Fleetwood is also a working sheep farm where Corriedales and white and silver-blue Lincolns are raised for wools prized by hand-spinners and fiber artists.

This inviting home has two guest rooms, each with air conditioning, fireplace, and private bath. The individually decorated rooms welcome guests with antique furnishings, coverlets and quilts, and fresh flowers. The grounds offer cook-out facilities, horseshoes, croquet, vegetable garden, and a Colonial herb garden. A canoe and fishing equipment are also available, and you can arrange for a picnic basket for special outings.

Breakfast is served to 9:30 a.m. in the dining room, where family silver and goblets glitter under a magnificent antique crystal chandelier. The table and leather-covered chairs, which belonged to Carol's mother, are duplicates of the chairs in the Governor's Palace in Williamsburg. A departing guest once echoed the sentiment of other visitors when he told Carol that Fleetwood was "just like coming to Grandma's house."

The B&B is well situated for trips to the nation's capital, 35 miles away, and Manassas Battlefield, just nine mile from Fleetwood. Other attractions in the area include historic mansions and gardens, shops, restaurants, riding stables, tennis, and swimming. Special events are scheduled year-round in historic Leesburg.

*I*NDIVIDUAL EGG AND SAUSAGE CASSEROLES

1 slice French bread, crust removed and cubed

2 ounces sausage, crumbled and browned

2 well-beaten eggs per ramekin

¼ cup shredded Cheddar cheese Tabasco sauce (do not use if sausage is hot and spicy)

1 teaspoon fresh chives, chopped

Spray 1 ramekin with cooking oil spray. Place one layer of bread cubes in each ramekin. Add a layer of sausage. Add a few drops of Tabasco sauce to the eggs if the sausage is mild. Pour the eggs over the sausage and bread to ½ inch from top. Sprinkle with the Cheddar cheese. Top with chives as desired. Bake immediately at 350° for 30 to 35 minutes. They will puff way up and be beautiful. Serve immediately.

SERVES 1.

Chef's Hint: Try a variety of sausage—venison, lamb, or pork. The casseroles can made up the night before, covered with foil, and refrigerated.

ORANGE GINGER PEARS

4 large canned pear halves	4 teaspoons raspberry jam
1/2 cup marmalade	8 strips crystallized ginger
1/4 cup orange juice	(optional)
1/4 teaspoon ground ginger	

In a shallow microwave dish, mix the marmalade and orange juice to form a medium to thick syrup. Place the pear halves in the syrup and spoon syrup over the pears. Sprinkle with ground ginger. Microwave on high for 2 minutes. Place a pear half in each dish; spoon some syrup over each, making sure to include pieces of orange. Sprinkle with ground ginger again. Spoon 1 teaspoon of raspberry jam across pear half. Top with narrow strips of crystallized ginger. Serve immediately, one pear half per person.

SERVES 4.

Chef's Note: Fleetwood Farm serves the pears in antique crystal dishes on individual plates with lace doilies and edible flowers from the garden.

Authors' Tip: The crystallized ginger may be omitted if desired.

 SEVEN HILLS INN

408 South Main Street • Lexington, Virginia 24450 • (540) 463-4715 • Jane Grigsby

The Seven Hills Inn, located in the heart of Lexington's historic Main Street district, is a classic white-columned, brick Southern Colonial dwelling. The inn's seven deluxe double rooms are each named for one of Rockbridge County's eighteenth- and nineteenth-century homesteads and farms. The tasteful decor includes fine antiques and hand-crafted reproductions.

The inn's convenient downtown location makes walking a pleasure. Located in the heart of the Shenandoah Valley and framed by the Blue Ridge and Allegheny Mountains, Lexington is the home of Washington and Lee University, the Virginia Military Institute, and the Virginia Horse Center. Handsomely preserved, the town is ideal for strolling and sightseeing. We recommend the Lexington Visitors Center's walking tour, which follows in the footsteps of distinguished residents Robert E. Lee and Thomas J. "Stonewall" Jackson.

Other nearby attractions include Natural Bridge, the Lime Kiln Theater, the farmstead of Cyrus McCormick, the Blue Ridge Parkway, recreational areas, and miles of beautiful country roads to explore.

CARAMEL FRENCH TOAST

Filling
- 8 ounces cream cheese
- 1 can condensed sweetened milk
- 1 teaspoon vanilla extract

Toast
- 1 cup firmly packed light brown sugar
- ½ cup butter (1 stick)
- 2 tablespoons light corn syrup

- 1½ cups whole milk
- 6 eggs
- 1 teaspoon vanilla extract
- ¼ teaspoon salt
- 12 slices white bread trimmed of crust
- Fruit and whipped cream for topping

To make the filling, in a medium bowl beat the cream cheese, condensed milk, and vanilla together and put in the refrigerator for about an hour, until it firms up.

In a heavy small saucepan, combine the brown sugar, butter, and corn syrup. Stir the mixture over medium-low heat until the butter melts and the sugar dissolves. Bring to a boil. Pour into 13x9x2-inch glass baking dish. Tilt dish to coat bottom evenly. Allow to cool.

Arrange 6 bread slices in a single layer atop sugar/syrup mixture. Spread the cream cheese mixture on top. Place remaining trimmed bread over mixture. In a small bowl, beat together the milk, eggs, vanilla, and salt and pour over the bread.

Bake uncovered at 350° until the bread is puffed and light golden brown, about 40 minutes. Let stand for 5 minutes. Cut into 6 portions. Using a spatula, invert each portion onto a plate so that the caramel faces up. Garnish with fruit and top with whipped cream.

MAKES 6 SERVINGS.

Chef's Hint: For fruit topping, use frozen cherry-berry blend partially thawed so the fruit still hold its shape.

THE INN AT THE CROSSROADS

Route 2, Box 6 R. R. 692 • North Garden, Virginia 22959 • (804) 979-6452 • Lynn Neville and Tee Neville Garrison

A charming four-story brick structure, The Inn at the Crossroads was built as a tavern to serve travelers bound for Richmond, from the Shenandoah Valley to the James River. The simple, Federal-style inn has many of the features of the "Ordinaries" or public houses of the period, including its long front porch. The guest rooms retain the feeling of their earliest days, and each room is decorated according to a theme that is carried out even in the books collected there. Guests are treated to a delicious full breakfast served in the Keeping Room.

North Garden is located nine miles south of Charlottesville, and visitors will find many fascinating attractions in the area including Thomas Jefferson's Monticello, James Monroe's Ash Lawn, Mitchie Tavern, Montpelier, and the University of Virginia. For recreation, you might try canoeing and tubing on the James River, cycling, skiing, or tennis—all available nearby. It's also an easy drive to the beautiful Blue Ridge Mountains and the Shenandoah Valley.

ERB-BAKED EGGS

4 eggs
1 teaspoon Dijon mustard
⅓ to ½ cup plain nonfat yogurt
¾ cup shredded Cheddar cheese

1 tablespoon chopped fresh chives
1 tablespoon chopped fresh parsley

Butter 4 ramekins. In a medium bowl beat the eggs, mustard, and yogurt. Stir in ¼ cup of the cheese. In a small bowl mix together the chives and parsley. Add half of the mixed herbs to the egg mixture. Stir well and spoon mixture into prepared ramekins. Sprinkle with the remaining cheese and herbs. Place the filled ramekins in a pan filled with about ½ inch of water. Bake at 350° for about 45 minutes or until firm and golden. Turn out onto serving plates. Garnish with sprigs of herbs. Serve immediately.

SERVES 4.

Chef's Note: This recipe has evolved from one of the first cookbooks I received as a new B&B owner. All my guests love it.

RAND MARNIER FRENCH TOAST

6 eggs
⅔ cups orange juice
⅓ cup Grand Marnier
⅓ cup milk
3 tablespoons sugar

¼ teaspoon vanilla extract
¼ teaspoon salt
Finely grated orange peel
10 ¾-inch-thick slices French bread

Un a bowl beat the eggs. Add the orange juice, Grand Marnier, milk, sugar, vanilla extract, salt, and orange peel. Dip both sides of the bread in the batter and lay them flat in an ungreased baking pan. Pour the batter over the bread, cover, and refrigerate overnight. Fry in a buttered skillet or on a griddle.

SERVES 4 OR 5.

Chef's Hint: Delicious made with homemade French bread and served with fresh blueberry sauce.

Chef's Note: This recipe was given to me by a friend in Boston. You may substitute more orange juice for the Grand Marnier if you prefer no alcohol.

Authors' Tip: Commercially prepared blueberry syrup also makes a delicious topping. This is an elegant recipe to serve overnight guests. All the preparation is done the night before—just fry the toast in the morning.

CRANBERRY ORANGE BREAD

2 cups all-purpose flour	1 cup coarse chopped cranberries
¾ cups sugar	1 teaspoon grated orange peel
1½ teaspoons baking powder	1 beaten egg
1 teaspoon salt	¾ cup orange juice
½ teaspoon baking soda	2 tablespoons salad oil

In a large bowl mix together the flour, sugar, baking powder, salt, baking soda, cranberries, and grated orange peel. In a separate bowl beat together the egg, juice, and oil. Add the egg mixture to the dry ingredients and stir until just moist. Pour into a greased loaf pan. Bake at 350° for 50 minutes.

MAKES 1 LOAF.

Chef's Hint: This recipe can easily be translated into a muffin recipe. Be sure to reduce the cooking time, however.

Chef's Note: This recipe has been my personal favorite since I received it in 1971 from a coworker at Massachusetts General Hospital.

$\mathscr{H}$IGH MEADOWS INN

Route 4, Box 6 • Scottsville, Virginia 24590 • (804) 286-2218 • Peter Sushka and Mary Jae Abbitt

$\mathscr{S}$ituated in Virginia's wine country, High Meadows is Virginia's only inn to combine its place on the National Register of Historic Places with a renaissance farm vineyard. The Federalist portion of the house was built by surveyor Peter White in 1832. Businessman Charles Harris added the Victorian portion some 50 years later. In 1905, lumber man W. F. Palette constructed the Queen Anne style Mountain Sunset Manor. This grand and unique inn welcomes guests with champagne. The accommodations are furnished with period art and antiques, and the innkeepers will show you their leather folio containing descriptions of the restoration. For nature-lovers, the fifty-acre estate includes gardens, footpaths, forests and ponds.

The inn's breakfast and dinner menus are carefully planned for today's health-conscious diners. Homemade breads, muffins and scones, gourmet egg dishes, and fresh fruits start the day. Multi-course dinners feature northern European and Mediterranean cuisines.

You will enjoy a stroll through Scottsville, which is listed on the National Register. The inn is also convenient to Appomattox, the presidential homes of

Monticello and Ash Lawn, and the Blue Ridge Parkway. Remember to ask about wine tastings at local wineries.

CHICKEN BREAST CITRON

6 chicken breast halves (deboned with skin left on)
1 cup freshly squeezed lemon juice (5 lemons)
1 cup freshly squeezed lime juice (7 limes)
¾ cup all-purpose flour
2 teaspoons paprika

Freshly cracked black pepper
¾ cup chicken stock
2 tablespoons light brown sugar
2 teaspoons herbes de Provence (found at gourmet grocery stores)
1 lemon, thinly sliced

At least 12 hours prior to brunch, place the chicken breast halves in a shallow dish (large enough to hold breasts in a single layer). Combine the lemon and lime juices and pour over the chicken. Marinate 12 hours, turning pieces occasionally. Remove chicken from the marinade, reserving the remainder. Combine the flour, paprika, and pepper. Dredge the chicken in the flour mixture and place each piece skin side up in a shallow, greased pan. Bake at 350° for 25 minutes. While the chicken is baking, place the remaining juices in a small saucepan. Add the chicken stock, brown sugar, and herbs. Heat to a boil, then set aside. After 25 minutes, lay a slice of lemon on each chicken piece and pour the sauce overtop. Return to the oven and bake 20 minutes more. Serve at once. Also excellent served cold.

SERVES 6.

$\mathcal{N}$O-KNEAD AND NEVER-FAIL HIGH MEADOWS BREAD

4⅓ cups whole-wheat and all-purpose white flour (about half and half)
2 packages active dry yeast
2 tablespoons honey

1¾ cups warm water (105° to 115°)
⅓ cup vegetable oil
1½ teaspoons salt
⅓ cup wheat germ

Put flour in a bowl and place in a warm, 150° oven for 15 minutes. In a large bowl dissolve the yeast and honey in ¾ cup of warm water and let stand until bubbly (5 to 15 minutes). Stir in remaining one cup of water, oil, salt, and wheat germ. Add the warmed flour 1 cup at a time, beating well by hand after each addition. When dough begins to cling to sides of bowl, turn onto floured board and shape into smooth loaf. Place in greased 9x5-inch loaf pan and cover with plastic wrap. Let rise in a warm place until 1 inch above the rim (35 minutes). Bake in a preheated 400° oven for 35 minutes.

MAKES 1 LOAF.

Chef's Hint: This bread is good served cold and sliced for sandwiches.

$\mathcal{B}$LACKBERRY ORANGE TEA BREAD

5 cups all-purpose flour
1 cup sugar
1 cup firmly packed brown sugar
2 tablespoons plus 1 teaspoon baking powder
2 teaspoons salt

2½ cups milk
2 eggs
2 cups blackberries
6 tablespoons oil
2 teaspoons vanilla extract
2 teaspoons grated orange peel

In a large bowl mix the flour, sugars, baking powder, and salt. Add the milk, eggs, berries, oil, vanilla, and orange peel. Pour into 2 greased loaf pans and bake at 350° for 1 hour.

MAKES 2 LOAVES.

BANANA STRAWBERRY BREAD

½ cup butter
1 cup sugar
2 eggs
2 cups mashed ripe bananas
1 tablespoon lemon juice

3 cups all-purpose flour
½ tablespoon baking powder
½ teaspoon salt
¾ cup strawberry jam
1 cup chopped pecans or walnuts

In a bowl cream the butter and gradually add the sugar, beating until fluffy. Add the eggs one at a time, beating after each addition. Combine bananas and lemon juice and stir into creamed mixture. Combine flour, baking powder, and salt. Add to creamed mixture and stir only until just moist. Stir in strawberry jam and nuts and spoon batter into 2 greased and floured loaf 9x4x3-inch loaf pans. Bake at 350° for 1 hour. Allow to cool for 10 minutes and remove from pans.

MAKES 2 LOAVES.

HIGH MEADOWS CLASSIC EGG CUP

2 slices ham (or Canadian bacon, turkey, etc.)
2 eggs
2 ounces grated Gruyère cheese

2 slices tomato
Fresh parsley or basil
2 slices of toast (optional)

Lightly grease 2 6-ounce ramekins or custard cups and gently press one slice of meat into each cup to form a surround. Break an egg into each meat ramekin and top each with 1 ounce grated cheese followed by one slice of tomato and parsley or basil. Bake at 350° for 20 minutes. Then with a knife lift the "egg cup" out of the baking cup and serve on its own or on a slice of toasted bread.

SERVES TWO.

ASPARAGUS EGG FRITTATA

3 tablespoons olive oil
1½ cups chopped fresh asparagus
⅓ cup mushrooms
1 clove garlic, minced
½ bell pepper, diced
¼ pound meat (chicken, turkey, ham, beef, salami) sliced into julienne strips
6 eggs, beaten

Pinch of salt
½ teaspoon freshly cracked black pepper
½ cup shredded cheese (Monterey Jack, Muenster, Swiss, or Cheddar)
¼ cup freshly grated Parmesan cheese

Heat the oil on medium heat in an 8½-inch skillet. Add the chopped asparagus, mushrooms, garlic, and bell pepper. Stir, cover, and cook 3 minutes. In a bowl combine the meat strips with the eggs, salt (to taste), pepper and shredded cheese. Remove the skillet from the heat and stir the vegetables into the egg mixture. Bake at 350° for 20 minutes. Top with Parmesan cheese and place under a broiler for 1 minute to brown.

SERVES 4 TO 5.

EASIEST TURKEY AND HAM TIMBALES

2 ounces cubed turkey, ham, or chicken
2 ounces sharp Cheddar cheese, shredded
2 to 3 eggs

½ cup milk
2 tablespoons chopped scallions
½ teaspoon paprika
½ teaspoon white pepper
1 teaspoon Parmesan cheese

Lightly grease 2 6-ounce custard cups and place the cubed meat and shredded cheese on the bottom of each cup. In a small bowl mix together the eggs, milk, scallions, paprika, and pepper and pour half into each custard cup on top of the meat and cheese. Top with the Parmesan cheese and bake at 375° for 30 minutes. Serve hot.

SERVES 2.

PECAN ORANGE MUFFINS

½ cup butter (1 stick) at room temperature
1 cup plus 1 tablespoon sugar
2 eggs
1 teaspoon baking soda
Peel of one orange, finely grated

2 cups all-purpose flour
1 cup plain yogurt or buttermilk
¾ cup chopped pecans
⅓ cup freshly squeezed orange juice
1 tablespoon sugar for topping

Grease 12 muffin cups. In a medium bowl, beat the butter and add sugar until creamy. Beat in the eggs. Stir in the baking soda and the grated orange peel. Fold in half the flour, then half the yogurt. Repeat, and then fold in the pecans. Scoop the batter into muffin cups. Bake at 375° for 20 to 25 minutes. Remove and brush orange juice over muffins and sprinkle with 1 tablespoon sugar.

MAKES 12 MUFFINS.

CHOCOLATE TORTONI

1 cup chilled whipped cream
½ cup chocolate-flavored syrup, chilled
¼ cup almond macaroon or vanilla extract wafer crumbs
¼ cup plus 2 tablespoons chopped almonds, divided

¼ cup chopped maraschino cherries
1½ tablespoons rum or ½ teaspoon rum extract
Whole maraschino cherries

Place the whippped cream in a small bowl. Gently fold in the chocolate syrup. Stir in the cookie crumbs, ¼ cup chopped almonds, chopped maraschino cherries, and rum or rum extract. Divide mixture into 4 dessert dishes and freeze until firm, about 4 hours. Just before serving, sprinkle with remaining chopped almonds and garnish with maraschino cherries.

SERVES 4.

CRANBERRY ALMOND MUFFINS

1½ cups all-purpose flour
½ cup sugar
1 teaspoon baking powder
¼ teaspoon baking soda
¼ teaspoon salt
2 eggs

¼ cup melted butter
½ cup sour cream
½ teaspoon almond extract
¾ cup sliced almonds
½ cup whole cranberry sauce

In a large bowl mix the flour, sugar, baking powder, baking soda, and salt. In another bowl break the eggs and whisk in the butter, sour cream, and almond extract. When blended, stir in the almonds. Pour the egg mixture over the dry ingredients and fold in until the dry ingredients are moistened. Grease a muffin tin. Spoon 2 tablespoons of batter into each greased muffin cup and top with a tablespoon of cranberry sauce. Sprinkle remaining batter with almonds and pour over the cranberry sauce. Bake at 375° for 30 to 35 minutes. Allow to cool 15 minutes before serving.

MAKES 10 MUFFINS.

SPICY SOUR CREAM AND RAISIN MUFFINS

2 eggs
½ cup sour cream
½ cup milk
2 tablespoons instant coffee
¾ cup raisins
1½ cups all-purpose flour

½ cup oatmeal
½ cup sugar
2 teaspoons baking powder
½ tablespoon each cinnamon, cloves, and allspice

Put the eggs, sour cream, milk, and instant coffee into a medium bowl. Whisk until well blended. Stir in the raisins. Let stand 5 minutes. Stir. Grease a muffin tin.

In a large bowl mix the flour, oatmeal, sugar, baking powder, and spices. Add the cream mixture and fold in until dry ingredients are moistened. Scoop batter into muffin cups. Sprinkle with oatmeal flakes. Bake at 375° for 20 to 25 minutes until browned. Serve hot.

MAKES 12 MUFFINS.

LEMON AND GINGER MUFFINS

½ cup butter (1 stick) at room
   temperature
1 cup sugar
2 eggs
2 tablespoons coarsely chopped
   ginger root
2 tablespoons freshly grated
   lemon peel

1 teaspoon baking soda
1 cup lemon yogurt
2 cups all-purpose flour
¾ cup golden raisins
¼ cup freshly squeezed lemon
   juice
2 tablespoons sugar

Grease muffin cups. In a large bowl, beat butter and one cup of sugar with a wooden spoon. Beat in the eggs 1 at a time. Add the ginger and the lemon peel. Stir baking soda into yogurt until it bubbles up. Fold flour into ginger-lemon mixture half at a time alternating with the yogurt. Add raisins. Put in prepared muffin cups and bake at 375° for 20 minutes. While the muffins are baking, combine the lemon juice with 2 tablespoons of sugar, stirring until the sugar is dissolved. Dip baked muffins, top and bottom, in the sugar and lemon juice mixture.

MAKES 12 MUFFINS.

Chef's note: This recipe was featured in *Chattanooga Times* food section in Chattanooga, Tennessee.

Authors' Tip: When we tried this recipe, the yield was 16 large muffins.

CREAMY BREAKFAST AMBROSIA

2 cups sliced peaches (or pears, apples, etc.)
2 bananas, sliced
10 to 12 strawberries, sliced
2 oranges, peeled and sliced
1 tablespoon lemon juice
1 cup shredded coconut
1 cup miniature marshmallows
1 cup vanilla or lemon yogurt
1 tablespoon sugar (optional)

In a large bowl, combine fruit and lemon juice. Toss lightly. Stir in coconut, marshmallows, yogurt, and sugar if desired. Chill for 30 minutes to 1 hour and serve in stemmed clear sherbet glasses.
SERVES 8.

HIGH MEADOWS INDIVIDUAL CHEESECAKES

1 pound 1% cottage cheese
¾ cup sugar
2 tablespoons cornstarch
¼ cup low fat buttermilk
¼ cup liquid nondairy creamer
¼ cup egg whites
¼ cup oil
1 teaspoon grated orange peel
1 teaspoon grated lemon peel
1 teaspoon vanilla extract
1 tablespoon lemon juice
Boiling water
Raspberry or strawberry sauce

Blend the cottage cheese in a food processor until smooth. Add the sugar, cornstarch, buttermilk, nondairy creamer, and egg whites. Again process and add oil with processor running. Finally, add the grated peels, vanilla extract, and lemon juice, and process for a few seconds. Divide into 6 to 8 ramekins or custard cups (about 8 ounces each). Place ramekins in a deep baking tray and pour boiling water into tray to a level slightly below the level of the cheese. Bake at 350° for 35 minutes. Remove, cool on a rack, then refrigerate. Serve with raspberry or strawberry sauce.
MAKES 6 TO 8 SERVINGS.

 THORNROSE HOUSE

531 Thornrose Avenue • Staunton, Virginia 24401 • (540) 885-7026 or (800) 861-4338
• Suzanne and Otis Huston

Thornrose House is a delightful turn-of-the-century Georgian Revival home embellished with a wraparound verandah and nearly an acre of gardens with Greek colonnades. A rose motif is carried throughout the house including the guest rooms. Rose colors prevail, and cabbage and English roses are part of the decor. The theme is carried into the garden, where roses are grown. The B&B stands adjacent to the 300-acre Gypsy Hill Park, which provides tennis, golf, and swimming facilities and summer band concerts.

Breakfast at Thornrose House begins with Bircher muesli, a tasty Swiss mixture of oats, fruits, nuts, and whipped cream. The rest of the menu is an ever-changing selection of delicious hot entrees and freshly baked muffins and breads.

Located in the heart of the Shenandoah Valley, the inn is convenient to the Blue Ridge National Park, Skyline Drive, The Museum of American Culture, Monticello, and a host of interesting historic sites, colleges, museums, summer theater, and fine restaurants. Staunton is a charming Victorian town with unique architecture. Its streets dip and wind following trails once used by Indians, stagecoaches, and wagon caravans.

OATMEAL WAFFLES WITH SPICED APPLES

1½ cups all-purpose flour
1 cup quick cooking oats
1 tablespoon baking powder
1 teaspoon cinnamon
¼ teaspoon salt

2 eggs, slightly beaten
1 cup milk
6 tablespoon butter, melted
2 tablespoons brown sugar
Spiced apples (recipe follows)

In a large mixing bowl, mix the flour, oats, baking powder, cinnamon, and salt. In a small mixing bowl stir together the eggs, milk, butter, and brown sugar. Add to the flour mixture all at once. Stir just until blended.

Put 1 to 1½ cups batter onto a preheated, lightly greased waffle iron. When done, remove with a fork. Top with spiced apples.

MAKES 4 WAFFLES.

SPICED APPLES

2 tablespoons unsalted butter, melted
2 cooking apples, peeled, cored, and thinly sliced
¼ cup pecan halves, toasted

1 tablespoon brown sugar
⅛ teaspoon cinnamon
⅛ teaspoon nutmeg
1 teaspoon vanilla extract

In a large skillet melt the butter and cook the apples over low heat, stirring occasionally, until tender. Add the pecans, brown sugar, cinnamon, nutmeg, and vanilla, tossing gently.

SERVES 4.

Authors' tip: Try adding a little apple juice to the apples while cooking.

*T*HORNROSE HOUSE BIRCHER MUESLI

1 cup whole oats
Milk
⅓ cup golden raisins
1 apple, cored and grated
Juice of ½ lemon

Chopped fruit of the season
2 large spoonfuls whipped cream
  or vanilla extract yogurt
⅛ cup toasted almonds

Soak the oats and raisins overnight in just enough milk to cover them. In the morning, add the grated apple, lemon juice, and fruit of the season. Fold in the whipped cream or vanilla yogurt and top with toasted almonds. Enjoy!

Serves 4 generously.

*A*NGEL BISCUITS

1 tablespoon active dry yeast
2 tablespoons lukewarm water
  (110° to 115°)
5 cups flour (unbleached or a
  combination of white and
  whole-wheat)

¼ cup sugar
3 teaspoons baking powder
1 teaspoon baking soda
1 teaspoon salt
1 cup shortening
2 cups buttermilk

To prepare the biscuits dissolve the yeast in warm water and set aside. Combine the flour, sugar, baking powder, soda, and salt in a large bowl. Cut in the shortening with a pastry cutter. Add the buttermilk and yeast mixture and mix well. Turn onto a floured board and knead gently 10 times. Roll dough to ½-inch thickness and cut with a biscuit cutter. Bake on an ungreased cookie sheet at 400° for 15 minutes.

Makes 24 3-inch rolls.

Chef's Note: This is a great and versatile recipe that can be made up the night before and refrigerated.

 CINNAMON ROLL VARIATION

3 tablespoons butter
1 cup brown sugar
⅔ cup chopped nuts
⅓ cup currants

1 teaspoon cinnamon
2 cups powdered sugar
4 to 6 tablespoons milk

To prepare the dough follow the instructions for preparation of the Angel Biscuits. Roll the dough into a large rectangle. Combine the butter, brown sugar, nuts, currants, and cinnamon and sprinkle over the dough. Carefully roll the dough, jellyroll fashion, and cut across making 1-inch rolls. Bake for 20 minutes. While still warm, drizzle with icing made of powdered sugar and 4 to 6 tablespoons of milk.

MAKES 18 ROLLS.

Chef's Note: This recipe variation comes from the Peach Tree Tea Room in Fredericksburg, Texas, and has made me look like I've been up all night just for my guests.

$\mathcal{S}$YCAMORE HILL HOUSE & GARDENS

Route 1, Box 978 • Washington, Virginia 22747 • (540) 675-3046 • Kerri and Stephen Wagner

$\mathcal{F}$ollow the mile-long driveway on Menefee Mountain, and it will take you to what may well be the only contemporary B&B in all of Virginia. Sited on a secluded 52-acre property, the inn is beautifully furnished and decorated with Kerri's exquisite flowers and plants, and Steve's original art. (Your innkeeper is also a well-known illustrator.) Here, you will enjoy comfortable rooms and gourmet food. Then you can settle into an Amish bentwood rocker on the 65-foot porch and be awestruck by the brilliant panoramic view of the Blue Ridge Mountains. Treat yourself to tea and home-baked cookies while you enjoy Kerri's gardens.

The village of Washington, which was laid out by young George Washington himself back in 1749, also boasts the well-known Inn at Little Washington and its superb (and expensive) restaurant. There are several excellent and more moderately priced restaurants in the area. You will also be close to a wide variety of sights and activities including the Skyline Drive, fishing, hiking, horseback riding and golfing facilities, caverns to explore, and antique and crafts stores to shop.

CINNAMON APPLE PUFF

1 very large tart apple (such as
  Granny Smith), peeled and
  sliced very thin
3 tablespoons butter
3 eggs
½ cup all-purpose flour

½ cup milk
1 teaspoon sugar
  Salt
2 tablespoons cinnamon-sugar
  Juice of 1 lemon

Liberally grease a 9-inch fluted quiche dish. Sauté the apple in 1 table-spoon butter until slightly tender. Spread the apple slices evenly in the quiche dish. In a bowl mix together the eggs, flour, milk, sugar, and salt until blended well and pour over apple slices. Bake at 475° for 10 minutes. Remove from oven, dot with remaining 2 tablespoons butter, and sprinkle with cinnamon-sugar. Return to the oven for 5 minutes. Bring to the table puffed, and sprinkle the lemon juice over the puff.

SERVES 4 WITH BREAKFAST ACCOMPANIMENTS.

SCALLOPED EGGS

3 tablespoons butter, divided
½ cup chopped green onion
6 large white mushrooms, sliced
  thin
8 eggs, beaten
½ teaspoon salt
¼ teaspoon pepper
2 to 3 fresh basil leaves chopped
  or ¼ teaspoon dried basil

1 tablespoon all-purpose flour
1 cup whole milk
½ cup grated Cheddar cheese
3 to 4 slices firm white bread
  (crusts removed), cut into
  small cubes

Melt 2 tablespoons of butter in a large skillet. Sauté the green onions and mushrooms until just tender. Add the eggs to skillet and scramble until eggs are just barely set. Spoon the mixture into a 9x9-inch greased baking dish and spread evenly. Sprinkle with salt, pepper, and basil. Melt remaining butter in the skillet and add the flour, milk, and cheese. Stir until thick and bubbly. Pour evenly over the egg mixture. Top with bread cubes. Bake at 325° for 35 to 45 minutes until bread is nicely browned. Serve with fresh fruit and pastries.

Serves 6.

*T*HICK SLICED FRENCH TOAST WITH SAUTÉED APPLES

French Toast
8 eggs
¼ teaspoon grated nutmeg
½ to ¾ cup half-and-half

Vegetable oil for frying (or cooking oil spray)
12 slices firm Italian bread, ¹⁄₁₂ inches thick

Whisk together the eggs, nutmeg, and half-and-half until well mixed. Heat a griddle to about 350° and spread the oil or spray evenly on surface or place a small amount of oil in a saucepan and heat to a medium high heat. Dip bread slices into egg-cream mixture, coating thoroughly, and fry in oil until browned evenly on both sides. Place in oven to hold on warm while preparing apples.

Sautéed apples
4 to 5 tablespoons butter
6 Granny Smith apples, cored, peeled, and thinly sliced

2 tablespoons cinnamon sugar

In a large skillet, melt the butter on medium heat. Add the apples and raise heat to medium high. Gently sauté apples for about 5 minutes, sprinkle with cinnamon sugar, and continue to sauté until apples are just tender. *Don't overcook.* Spoon apples over the French Toast. Serve with real maple syrup and freshly squeezed orange juice.

SERVES 6.

WILLIAMSBURG SAMPLER

922 Jamestown Road • Williamsburg, Virginia 23185 • (804) 253-0398 • Helen and Ike Sisane

This stately eighteenth-century plantation-style brick home was built on the site of the original Jamestown Road, the old byway that is marked on the "Frenchman's Map of 1782." The inn is typical of colonial times. The Sisanes have collected the furniture and accessories at auctions, estate sales, and as gifts from friends and relatives. Antiques, pewter items, and samplers are displayed throughout the house. Ask the Sisanes to tell you about their collection; the stories are fascinating.

Visits to the Williamsburg Sampler always begin with a memorable breakfast. You will wake to the fresh smells of brewing coffee and baking muffins. Then gather in the Ethan Allen dining room for a leisurely Skip Lunch breakfast served on fine china with pewter accents.

The sights and sounds of Colonial Williamsburg are just a short walk from the inn. And there's no place that captures the history of life in America's early days more completely than this superb restoration of Virginia's first capital. Every street is a trip into the 18th century and its craft shops, taverns, homes, businesses, and colonial entertainments.

FRENCH BREAKFAST PUFFS

2 tablespoons plus 2 teaspoons shortening
¼ cup sugar
½ egg
¾ cup all-purpose flour
¼ teaspoon salt
¾ teaspoon baking soda
⅛ teaspoon nutmeg
¼ cup milk
2 tablespoons butter
3 tablespoons sugar
½ teaspoon cinnamon

Cream together the shortening, sugar and egg. Combine the flour, salt, baking soda, and nutmeg. Add the milk to the creamed mixture and mix with the flour mixture. Fill greased muffin cups half full. Bake at 350° for 20 minutes. Melt 2 tablespoons butter in microwave. Combine the sugar and cinnamon in a bowl. Roll the puffs in the melted butter, then in the cinnamon-sugar mixture.

MAKES 6 PUFFS.

THE FAMOUS "SKIP LUNCH" BREAKFAST BISCUITS

1 egg
1 3-ounce package cream cheese
¼ cup sugar
¼ or ½ cup raisins
1 package Pillsbury Biscuit dough

In a bowl beat together the egg, cream cheese, sugar, and raisins. Pat the biscuit dough into 3-inch squares and arrange on an ungreased cookie sheet. Place a spoonful of the cheese and raisin mixture on each flattened biscuit. Bring the 4 corners together and bake on a cookie sheet at 400° for 12 to 15 minutes.

Makes 8 biscuits.

CHOW MEIN NOODLE COOKIES

1 6-ounce package butterscotch
  chips
½ cup peanut butter

1 3-ounce can chow mein
  noodles

Melt the butterscotch chips in the top of a double boiler. Stir in the peanut butter. Pour the melted mixture over the noodles. Drop by teaspoonfuls onto a cookie sheet lined with waxed paper. Chill.

MAKES 30 COOKIES.

THE MANOR AT TAYLOR'S STORE

Route 1, Box 533 • Wirtz, Virginia 24184 • (703) 721-3951 • Lee and Mary Lynn Tucker

Skelton Taylor, a First Lieutenant in Virginia's Bedford Militia, established Taylor's Store as a general merchandise trading post in 1799. The structure later served as an "ordinary" and a U.S. Post Office. The manor house was built in the early 1800s as the focus of a prosperous tobacco plantation.

One of the most satisfying features of a stay at The Manor nowadays is the full, heart-healthy breakfast included in your rates. With advance notice, the Tuckers will be happy to accommodate any special dietary preferences and restrictions.

The estate, set in the picturesque foothills of the Blue Ridge Mountains, includes 120 acres for hiking, and six spring-fed ponds. You can swim from the docks, sun on decks, canoe, fish, or just laze and watch the resident geese in these private places. Nearby Smith Mountain Lake also offers boating, fishing, and swimming, as well as golf and tennis, and delicious dining. From The Manor you have only a 20-minute drive to the Blue Ridge Parkway and

Roanoke. Other places that might catch your fancy are Mabry Mill, the Peaks of Otter, Roanoke's Mill Mountain Zoo, Farmer's Market, Mill Mountain Theater, and the Center in the Square.

VIRGINIA HAM BREAKFAST SOUFFLÉ

1 pound Virginia ham sausage or turkey sausage
4 green onions, chopped
1 to 2 cloves garlic, minced
2 8-ounce cartons of egg substitute
1 cup skim milk
¼ teaspoon ground red pepper
¾ teaspoon dry mustard
6 slices whole-wheat bread, cubed
Cooking oil spray

In a large skillet cook the sausage, onion, and garlic until the sausage is browned. Stir until the sausage crumbles, then drain. Rinse with hot water. Drain well and press between layers of paper towels. Set aside.

In a large bowl combine the egg substitute, skim milk, pepper, and mustard. Stir in the sausage mixture and the bread cubes. Spoon into 10 6-ounce ramekins or custard cups coated with cooking oil spray. Cover and chill 8 hours. Remove from the refrigerator 30 minutes before baking. Bake uncovered at 350° for 30 minutes or until set. Serve immediately.

SERVES 10.

Chef's Note: All our breakfasts are "heart healthy." This recipe was featured in the May, 1993, issue of *Southern Living* magazine in its write-up of the Manor at Taylor's Store.

WHOLE GRAIN PANCAKES

1 cup whole-wheat flour
2 tablespoons baking powder
2 tablespoons sugar
½ teaspoon allspice
¼ teaspoon nutmeg

2 egg whites, lightly beaten
1 cup skim milk
2 tablespoons vegetable oil
Fresh strawberries and thinly
sliced ham for garnish

In a medium bowl combine the flour, baking powder, sugar, allspice, and nutmeg. Make a well in center of the mixture. Combine the egg whites, milk, and oil. Add to the dry ingredients, stirring just until dry ingredients are moistened. Let stand 20 minutes.

For each pancake, spoon about 2 tablespoons batter onto a moderately hot griddle coated with cooking spray. Turn over the pancakes when the tops are covered with bubbles and the edges look cooked. Garnish with fresh strawberries and ham.

MAKES 8 TO 10 PANCAKES.

Chef's Note: This recipe appeared in *Southern Living* magazine.

 INDEX

Index